To Steffie and Fran

Dr. Pascal is also author of BEHAVIORAL CHANGE IN THE CLINIC—A SYSTEMATIC APPROACH *and (with Barbara J. Suttell)* THE BENDER GESTALT TEST—QUANTIFICATION AND VALIDITY FOR ADULTS.

Systematic Observation of
Gross Human Behavior

G. R. PASCAL AND W. O. JENKINS

Professors of Psychology
University of Tennessee

New York   **Grune & Stratton**   London

Library of Congress Catalog Card No.: 61-9412
Printed and Bound in the U.S.A. (B)

157
P26s

Contents

106717

Preface

It is a commentary on the state of affairs in psychology that a student interested in human behavior as it occurs in life is not considered a student of the science of psychology. Rather he is lightly exposed to "basic science" courses, given a large dose of technique courses, labeled "clinical" and relegated to those who practice psychology and not considered scientists. In spite of lip service to Watson, it seems as if psychology and the science of human behavior are considered mutually exclusive. It seems to us that a great many psychologists have not grasped that the scientific method can be applied to human behavior as it occurs in life situations (*sic*, Watson). Rather, they have confined themselves to the safer study of segmental responses, infrahuman organisms and tests and questionnaires. It seems to us that the time has come for psychology to broaden its perspective and provide systematic knowledge as a basis for the practice of clinical psychology and psychiatry.

Much research at the infrahuman level and methodological developments at the human level have provided the bases for at last coming to grips with the ultimate goal of psychology as a science, namely, the prediction of individual human behavior as it occurs in its natural habitat. This book attempts to provide a theoretical position and a method for gathering data about human behavior in life situations.

The failure of many departments of psychology to accept clinical psychology within the framework of the science of behavior may be attributed to the behavior of many practitioners of psychology, psychiatry and allied disciplines. They often speak and write as if the knowledge that we are only begining to accumulate has already been encompassed.

We believe that students of psychology who are now being

"shunted" into clinical psychology because of their interest in gross human behavior should be exposed to *more* rigorous training in the scientific method than students of classical experimental psychology. The study of gross human behavior is so difficult that it requires the highest standards of training. Failure to provide such training has resulted in a welter of studies impossible of replication. To counteract such a situation it is necessary that departments of psychology accept the study of gross human behavior (as we shall define it) as a legitimate area of scientific inquiry. We feel that those students who are now being side-tracked into "clinical" should be encouraged to become scientists in the field of gross human behavior.

Systematic knowledge about gross human behavior is as necessary for a science of psychology as is, for instance, knowledge of the gross behavior of molecules in chemistry. Such knowledge is propaedeutic to narrower studies in psychology. We need to know more than we do now concerning variables of gross human behavior that may bias laboratory data, and we should be able to specify the limiting characteristics of human organisms as we do for infrahuman organisms. These limiting characteristics are subtle and, for the most part, unrealized, e.g., does the 18 year old son "need" to leave home (as does the male anthropoid) or is he having "trouble" with his parents? A further benefit to be derived from considering the study of gross human behavior as propaedeutic to a science of psychology lies in the feed-back from accumulated data, and problems encountered, to theory and laboratory investigations.

We think that the approach presented in this book should be offered to the serious student of psychology early in his academic career. In our experience, a student coming to us to study psychology is primarily interested in human behavior as it occurs in life situations. This initial interest seems to be most reasonable and should be utilized to encourage the student to become a behavioral scientist. Such a student, swamped with a plethora of isolated facts that have little bearing on his initial interest, is more often than not discouraged from continuing with psychology. We have found little difficulty in teaching the theoretical position and a grasp of the methodology to advanced undergraduate students. They have been able to collect data for certain circumscribed areas such as sleeping behavior, eating and frequency of contact with parents. A recent upper-division class in personality contrasted Displays of Affection exhibited by parents toward male and female offsprings, collecting the data by the interview method. Their contact with, and systematic study of, other human beings gave concrete meaning to the study of personality, a respect for the complexities of gross human behavior and a healthy regard for the difficulties of methodology.

We wish to acknowledge, with gratitude, the contributions of our graduate students. To Drs. M. Zax, H. Salzberg and W. E. Morris our thanks for reading and commenting on the manuscript. To our colleagues at the Psychological Service Center of the University of Tennessee, Drs. K. R. Newton, C. N. Sipprelle and C. H. Swensen, Jr., we are indebted for their constant encouragement and stimulation. We express our thanks to the administration of the University of Tennessee, especially Professor E. E. Cureton, Head of the Department of Psychology.

To secretaries, Edith Coppinger, Catherine Davis and Carol Hammond, we express our gratitude for their patience and efforts.

Acknowledgement is made to the *Quarterly Journal of Studies on Alcohol* for permission to abstract from tables in an article by the authors.

Knoxville, Tennessee   G. R. P.
                                                    W. O. J.

Introduction 1

Man's reaction to his environment has been of concern to man since time immemorial. Zilboorg (1941) quotes Protagoras as saying, "man is the measure of all things." It occurs to us that man first placed the correlates of behavior outside himself, in the heavenly bodies, later deified. There was a gradual movement of the behavioral correlates closer to himself, the sea, the wind, the vapors. This movement continued until the correlates of behavior were placed inside man and Descartes was able to write *cogito ergo sum.* The emphasis has not changed to this day. The search for neural correlates of behavior goes on apace, far outdistancing the experiential correlates.

The search for behavioral correlates has resulted in little systematic knowledge about man's *reactions* to *stimuli* in his *natural environment!* This lack of knowledge becomes brutally apparent when one considers that man's reactions to other people as stimuli are no different today from the reactions of Cro-Magnon man! Predictability of behavior and the wherewithal to change it come from systematic observation. When man is the object of study this systematic knowledge is difficult to obtain. Perhaps it has required all these centuries to acquire the toughness to stand off and view man's behavior as a natural phenomenon, just as natural as the movement of the planets and stars. It may be that it has taken all this time for the development of a discipline that insists that, not the "humors," not the feelings, not the attitudes, not the soul of man be studied, but his observable reactions. *What does he do in response to what observable stimuli?*

We do not mean to imply that man's reactions to various kinds of stimuli have not been studied. Quite the contrary!

Many disciplines have been concerned with man's reaction to stimuli. Physiology, biochemistry, biology, and through these disciplines, medicine, have looked for the "causes" of behavior within the organism. At the other extreme, there have been disciplines concerned with the political, economic, social and cultural correlates of behavior. Psychology has taken man to the laboratory, studying his reactions to carefully controlled stimulus conditions. None of these disciplines, with the possible exception of cultural anthropology, has systematically studied man, during his life span, in his natural habitat. The approach to be presented in this book is concerned with just that, the reactions of man to stimuli in his natural environment.

The object of study of the approach to be presented is the intact human organism, his grossly observable responses to detectable stimulus conditions. The concern is with the life span of the individual organism. The entire emphasis of the approach is on acquired behavior, holding genetic factors constant, within broad limits. We are interested in the gross behavior of the human organism, behavior that has, so to speak, a "naked eye" effect on the environment. On the stimulus side we are interested in grossly observable environmental events that covary with detectable behavior. It is from considerations such as these that the term "gross human behavior" derives. The approach can be considered a variety of stimulus-response psychology with the emphasis on gross human behavior as it occurs outside the laboratory during the life span of the individual.

The sources of this approach are many and varied. One can find in the very early history of man statements that, at least indirectly, express belief in the later effects on behavior of early stimulus-response relationships, e.g., "as the twig is bent . . ." More directly and more immediately, however, we can discern at least three major antecedents: the works of Freud and his followers, cultural anthropologists and behavioristic psychologists. We shall, briefly, consider each of these influences.

It is our belief that Freud's greatest contribution lies in establishing, clinically, the relationship between early experience and later behavior in the human organism (1924). Although many others may be said to have antedated Freud (Zilboorg, 1941), none attempted to systematize the relationship and no one used this knowledge in practice. It was Freud who pointed out the necessity for studying early stimulus-response relationships in the life of an individual in order to predict and change adult behavior. Further, Freud, as a result of clinical practice, stated and restated the significance of specific, early stimulus-response relationships for later behavior.

Today, the psychoanalytic movement seems to be essentially based on this great contribution of Freud's. And, indeed, psychoanalytic psychotherapy of the "orthodox" type seems to be entirely directed toward exhuming early stimulus-response relationships! For our position, Harry Stack Sullivan's extension of Freud's original observations are most pertinent. His approach bears directly on our own (Sullivan, 1953). Sullivan attempted to conceptualize the nature of experience in a systematic fashion. He insisted that the "dynamic patterns of interaction" must be known both specifically and generally. In our approach, we have attempted to give specific and objective definition to concepts developed by Freud and extended by Sullivan. We have tried to translate these into stimulus-response terms.

Many workers since Freud have contributed to knowledge in the area of the effects of early experience on later behavior. The literature in this area is voluminous and any review of it, here, would be inappropriate. We have merely singled out what seems to us to be the chief psychoanalytic influences which bear on our approach.

The second identifiable source to the approach to be presented in this book stems from cultural anthropology. Investigators in this field have been concerned with behavioral differentials as a function of culture. In studying the effect of culture, they have, of necessity, gathered historical material about individuals. They have typically gathered information about cross-sectional behavior as well as early experiences. Data gathered by cultural anthropologists have made a great contribution to our understanding of human behavior. Thus, investigators like Linton (1936), Malinowski (1941), Mead (1949) and Sapir (1948) have provided data bearing on the relationship between early experiences and later behavior. However, their influence on our approach is not so much the data obtained but their methods of obtaining the data. This methodology is illustrated nicely in a recent book by Whiting and Child (1953).

The main source of our approach to the study of human behavior comes from "objective" psychologists such as Watson (1919), Smith and Guthrie (1921) and Hunter (1928) who emphasized the importance of learning in behavior. Although Watson and Hunter are the two most direct antecedents for the authors in their present approach, the idea that behavior is largely a function of experiences after birth is old. Locke uses Aristotle's notion of the *tabula rasa,* making it, as Boring (1929) writes, central to his whole system of psychology. Even before Locke, Hobbes had in 1651 written in his *Leviathan* that man in his natural state is "solitary, poor, nasty, brutish and short." The impact of Watson, dating from his article in the *Psychological Review* in 1913 was almost as if these ideas had never been advanced! In 1919, Watson wrote in the first page of his book:

Psychology is that division of natural science which takes human activity and conduct as its subject matter. It attempts to formulate through systematic observation and experimentation the laws and principles which underlie man's reactions. Every one agrees that man's acts are determined by something, and that, whether he acts orderly or not, there are sufficient grounds for his acting as he does act, if only these grounds can be discovered. In order to formulate such laws, we must study man in action—his adjustments to the daily situations of life, and to the unusual situations which may confront him.

Elsewhere, Watson writes (Hunter, 1953):

The general goal of behaviorism, then, is to so amass observations upon human behavior that in any given case, given the stimulus (or better, situation), the behaviorist can predict in advance what the response will be; or, given the response, he will be able to state what situation is calling out the reaction. Looked at in this broad way, it is easy to see that behaviorism is far away from its goal. But while its problems may be difficult, they are not insuperable.

The essentials of our approach are contained in Watson's statements, particularly that portion dealing with the need to observe, systematically, the behavior of people in their natural habitat. Watson's message concerning the study of *human* behavior finds its most direct expression in the writings of Hunter. In his *Human Behavior*, 1928, Hunter suggested a new discipline to be called "anthroponomy" which would be concerned with the study of man in his natural environment. He writes [1928, p. 3]:

... Most of the work on behavior utilizes relatively gross and obvious stimuli which can be applied to definite sense organs, receptors. In the same manner, the behavior which is observed is usually the obvious changes in the activity of the muscles of speech, of the hands, of the legs, and other readily observable portions of the body.

A number of later workers have espoused the behavioristic approach to the study of human behavior, such as Hull (1943), Tolman (1942) and Skinner (1953). Other workers have actually observed, systematically, human behavior. Investigators such as Barker (1954), Levy (1958), the Gluecks (1934), Sears et al. (1957), Flanagan (1954), Dollard and Miller (1950), Murray (1938) and Kinsey et al. (1948), have conducted studies of human behavior. Although our focus is broader than that of the workers cited, these must be considered as antecedents to our approach.

The basic approach of our book is not new to animal studies, particularly those studies dealing with the effects of early experiences on later behavior. Beach and Jaynes (1954) summarize much of this work in their comprehensive review paper. Many animal studies have used the longitudinal approach. This approach has been very rewarding in studies of the later effects of early deprivation. An excellent review covering both the animal and human literature in the area of sensory deprivation has been written by Wheaton (1959).

It may seem to the reader that these are widely divergent sources for a systematic approach such as ours. However, the differences between these various sources are more apparent than real. Let us, for instance, take the two seemingly most disparate positions, Freud's and Watson's. Freud emphasized the effects of early experience on later behavior. Although his theoretical statements make much of constitutional factors, his practice of psychoanalysis is primarily concerned with the reinstatement (abreaction) of early experiences and the connection between these and the patient's current behavior. It seems to us that Freud espoused the effects of learning experiences on later behavior. Freud's position with respect to changing human behavior can, then, be restated in stimulus-response terms. Freud's practical interest lay in the behavioral characteristics of the stimuli (parents, siblings, and others) encountered by the patient and the patient's responses to them. Early stimulus-response relationships uncovered by Freud in the process of psychoanalysis were deemed by him to be the bases for later responses to similar stimulus situations. Watson wrote "Psychology . . . attempts to formulate through systematic observation and experimentation the laws and principles which underlie man's reactions" (*ibid*). Watson, also, emphasized the importance of early stimulus-response relationships for later behavior. Freud, in his practice, systematically observed stimulus-response relationships in the life span of the individual. Watson defined the science of psychology in these terms!

Building on these various sources we have attempted a systematic approach to the observation of human behavior as it occurs in day-to-day situations over the life span of the individual. The subject matter of this approach we have called *gross human behavior*. In this book, we begin by presenting our systematic position in detail. We then go on to define what we mean by stimuli and responses. Next, techniques of systematic observation are presented. There follow, then, definitions of stimulus and response variables and their basic measures. Together, these comprise our Behavioral Scales which are the specific guides for observing human behavior. Thereafter, a section of the book is devoted to methodological considerations and investigations in which the scales are actually used. Finally, illustrative material is included in the Appendices to clarify methodology.

REFERENCES

Barker, R. G., and Wright, H. F.: Midwest and its Children. White Plains, New York, Row, Peterson and Co., 1954.

Beach, F. A., and Jaynes, J.: Effects of early experience upon the behavior of animals. Psychol. Bull. *51:* 239-264, 1954.

Boring, E. G.: A History of Experimental Psychology. New York, Century, 1929.

Dollard, J., and Miller, N. E.: Personality and Psychotherapy. New York, McGraw-Hill, 1950.

Flanagan, J. C.: The critical incident technique.. Psychol. Bull. *51:* 327-358, 1954.

Freud, S.: Collected Papers. London, Hogarth Press, 1924.

Glueck, S., and Glueck, E.: One Thousand Juvenile Delinquents. Cambridge, Harvard Univ. Press, 1934.

Hull, C. L.: Principles of Behavior. New York, Appleton-Century, 1943.

Hunter, W. S.: Human Behavior. Chicago, Univ. Chicago Press, 1928 (rev. ed.).

—: Behaviorism. Encycl. Brit., 1953.

Kinsey, A. C., Pomeroy, W. B., and Martin, C. E.: Sexual Behavior in the Human Male. Philadelphia, Saunders, 1948.

Levy, D. M.: Behavioral Analysis. Springfield, Ill., Thomas, 1958.

Linton, R.: The Study of Man. New York, Appleton-Century, 1936.

Malinowski, B.: The Sexual Life of Savages. New York, Halcyon, 1941.

Mead, M.: Male and Female. New York, Morrow, 1949.

Murray, H. A. et al.: Explorations in Personality. New York, Oxford Univ. Press, 1938.

Sapir, E.: In Mandelbaum, D., Ed.: Selected Writings in Language Culture and Personality. Berkeley, Univ. Calif. Press, 1948.

Sears, R. R., Maccoby, E. E., and Levin, H.: Patterns of Child Rearing. White Plains, N. Y., Row, Peterson & Co., 1957.

Skinner, B. F.: Science and Human Behavior. New York, MacMillan, 1953.

Smith, S., and Guthrie, E. R.: General Psychology in Terms of Behavior. New York, Appleton, 1921.

Sullivan, H. S.: Interpersonal Theory of Psychiatry. New York, Norton, 1953.

Tolman, E. C.: Drives toward War. New York, Appleton-Century, 1942.

Watson, J. B.: Psychology from the Standpoint of a Behaviorist. Philadelphia, Lippincott, 1919.

Wheaton, J. L.: Fact and Fancy in Sensory Deprivation Studies. School of Aviation Medicine, Brooks A.F.B., Tex. Review, 5-59, August, 1959.

Whiting, J. W. M., and Child, I. L.: Child Training and Personality: A Cross-Cultural Study. New Haven, Yale Univ. Press, 1953.

Zilboorg, G.: A History of Medical Psychology. New York, Norton, 1953.

Systematic Position 2

Any response of the human organism is a function of a complexity of factors, some of which can be identified. A given response covaries with the immediately identifiable stimulus situation such as another person, other aspects of the biologic and physical environment, the constitution and physical condition of the responding person and his past history. These independent variables lend themselves to a schematic continuum of stimuli impinging on the person ranging from those within the organism to those remote from it, from a cortical lesion to solar disturbances. Of these independent variables our focus is on those stimuli covarying with behavior that are *outside* the organism. Our systematic position postulates an "empty" organism (Boring, 1946; Skinner, 1938). Our interest lies in grossly observable stimuli outside the organism that have measurable behavioral correlates. This is a systematic position, not a denial of the interior of the organism. For other systematic approaches the interior of the organism is the main focus.

In postulating the empty organism, we do not wish to imply that we are indifferent to individual differences based on, for instance, constitution. For given stimuli there will be gross variation of responses. Levels of responding will accrue to individuals who then can be differentiated on the basis of these responses. Thus, there will be a set of responses characteristic of, let us say, an idiot. Another set of responses will be characteristic of a physicist. A person with a cortical lesion is identified not on the basis of anatomic and physiologic considerations but, rather, on the basis of responses to stimuli outside the organism. The interior of the organism covaries with behavior, but is outside the realm of our systematic position. The point we wish to make is that from our position individuals are differentiated on the basis of responses to stimuli outside the organism.

This stimulus-response position is held by many psychologists, sociologists, cultural anthropologists, political economists and other students of behavior. The sociologists are interested in the behavior of groups of individuals based on correlated social conditions, such as crime. The cultural anthropologists and political economists are also interested in the behavior of groups of peoples. Psychology is interested in individual human behavior. Individual human behavior is systematically observed in the psychological laboratory. In psychological research, there is continuum of specificity of stimulus and response ranging from the reaction of a single nerve fiber to an electrical stimulus to responses of large groups of people to others. Neither of these extremes is of concern to us.

The present approach is concerned with the behavior of the intact human organism in response to environmental stimuli. The stimuli of special interest are people. Our focus lies in man's reactions to his natural habitat. Of these reactions, we study the grossly detectable responses of the intact individual organism during his life span. Thus, in a cross-sectional, or longitudinal, study we would measure the approach-avoidance behavior of a male subject in response to female peers. We would not measure his galvanic skin response. However, we would record grossly detectable sweating. The focus of study is consistent behavior displayed in response to stimuli encountered by the individual in day-to-day living. For want of a better word we have labeled the behavior of interest to us, "gross." The word is to be taken in its modern meaning of entire or total, or in its archaic meaning of plain, evident or obvious.

If one is interested in human behavior as it occurs in life situations, it is necessary to begin by systematically observing such behavior. The naturalistic observation of human behavior begins with the study of reactions and accompanying environmental conditions. This is the descriptive stage of scientific development. Continued observation of this sort leads to hypotheses that certain behaviors occur with given frequencies.

A later stage of observation may then lead to hypotheses about the environmental conditions under which the behavior occurs. For instance, a man lies down, becomes immobile, closes his eyes, and breathes regularly. This behavior is noted to occur with a given frequency. Then it is observed that the behavior is exhibited under a certain set of environmental conditions, namely, when it is dark. It is hypothesized that the behavior in question is related to the condition of darkness. When this hypothesis is tested, covariation is demonstrated between the behavior described and the condition of darkness. However, in the process of further observation, it is discovered that the behavior described begins with varying lapses of time from the onset of darkness. Obviously, other variables need to be discovered which might covary with this new observation. Such a state of affairs requires the collection of more data about environmental conditions. Various variables such as height of the tide, presence or absence of the moon, etc. are observed, but no consistent relationship is found between them and the time lag between the onset of darkness and the behavior described (sleep). Eventually, temperature is found to covary with the time lag between onset of darkness and sleep. Now we have two variables both of which seem to be related to the onset of sleeping behavior. However, these are not perfect predictors of sleeping behavior under all conditions. Other variables, such as number of hours of sleep deprivation, need to be observed and measured before more accurate predictions can be made.

The point we wish to make is that systematic observation at the purely descriptive level is fundamental to the detection of consistent covariation between environmental and behavioral events. This process, in turn, is the basis for testable hypotheses. Only in this way can the study of human behavior as it occurs in nature become scientific. It is noteworthy that psychology, the science of behavior, has not, at the human level, followed this approach. In this respect, it has differed from the other natural sciences. The reasons for this lack are many and complex and outside the realm of our discussion. It is intriguing, however, that although the approach has been applied to animal behavior through the anthropoid ape, it has not reached the level of human behavior.

Our approach deals with events external to the organism. We are only interested in environmental events and the organism's reactions to them. We are aware, of course, that stimuli are defined in terms of a response of some organism, the observed or the observer. It follows, therefore, that there are a number of stimuli not measurable with this approach. Although behavior takes place in a stimulus context, there are many behaviors for which the eliciting stimuli are not readily apparent. These behaviors we have called "operant," following Skinner (1938). Despite the lack of stimulus specificity in some behaviors, the stimulus context can be described and stimulus context-response relationships established. The emphasis of this systematic position on stimuli external to the organism and covarying behaviors in the natural environment differentiates it from clinical and traditional personality approaches.

Information in this area is not easily acquired, and the problems of measurement are staggering. Ideally, to obtain the information we are interested in, one would have to make consistent observations of stimulus-response events from birth onward. To obtain the most valid data at any cross-sectional level, one would have to maintain consistent contact with the subject and yet remain unobserved in order not to bias the data. One would have to be an invisible man with an extremely long life span in order to obtain any appreciable amount of information. However, there are ways to approximate the data of interest. Techniques are available which provide some estimate of the data. It is possible to observe some of the behavior and other data can be obtained by verbal report of the subject and others who have observed him. The important point is the nature of the verbal report. The "behavioral incident," which we shall discuss at length in a later section, is the key to obtaining valid data.

All science begins with crude observations. Thus, in physics, electricity was known and used with little knowledge of it. Molecules were bandied about with no knowledge of nuclear physics. Astronomy's first crude observations led to navigational aids. In our own field, circus trainers achieved remarkable results in the training of their animals without benefit of modern learning principles. In the example cited previously, knowledge that sleep covaried with darkness was a crude predictor of sleeping behavior without measurement of other variables related to sleep. Thus, in the field of gross human behavior we are certain that, however crude the measures, predictive principles will emerge. To obtain these predictive principles the basic observations must be made.

There will be many objections to this approach to the study of gross human behavior. It does not involve any particular instrumentation, and precise measurement is definitely lacking. The chief instrument is the fallible human observer. There is no alternative if we are to begin the scientific study of man. Arm chair philosophy, clinical anecdotes and segmental studies cannot provide the bases for the measurement and prediction of gross human behavior.

REFERENCES

Boring, E. G.: Mind and mechanism. Am. J. Psychol. 59: 173-192, 1946.
Skinner, B. F.: The Behavior of Organisms. New York, Appleton-Century, 1938.

The Stimulus Situation 3

The definition of the stimulus has always been a problem in behavioral science. Lewin (1936) dealt with this problem in his concept of the life space. Koffka (1935) made a distinctition between the geographical and psychological enviroment. For Tolman (1949), the stimulus situation is the form in which any immediate environment is perceived and/or remembered and/or inferred by the organism at a given time. For Hebb (1949) the chief characteristic of the stimulus situation is whether or not it activates the central nervous system. Both Guthrie (1935) and Hull (1943) lay heavy emphasis on afferent neural activity in their definition of the stimulus. In contradistinction to these theorists, Skinner (1953) has placed greater emphasis on the physical characteristics of the stimulus external to the organism. None of these conceptions of the stimulus exactly meet the needs of the present systematic approach.

Stimulus situations range from those that can be fairly precisely described to those that are extremely difficult in our present state of knowledge. At our level of discourse, there seems to be little difficulty in defining the stimulus when a nerve fiber reacts to an electrical impulse. Within the limits of the known properties of nerve fibers there is a one-to-one correspondence between stimulus and response. As soon as we get to the intact organism, however, the stimulus is not so easily definable. For instance, what are the stimuli for movements of a satiated albino rat in a maze for the first time? Curiosity drive? Such a concept has no status in our approach to gross behavior. In the particular case in question, a satiated rat in a maze, we cannot specify the specific stimuli which trigger off the rat's movements. We can, however, describe the maze, the general environment and the experimenter's behavior. In so doing, we still will not know what particular properties of the total stimulus situation are related to the responses of the rat. The problem becomes even more complicated when we consider man operating in his natural environment. What are the stimuli for the behavior of the experimenter introducing a rat into a maze? We can describe the laboratory situation ad infinitum, but the particular characteristics of the immediately observable stimuli directly eliciting the experimenter's behavior elude us.

It seems appropriate, at this point, to consider a distinction between a stimulus and a stimulus situation. This problem is not new with us but seems particularly pertinent to our approach and needs to be discussed before we go on with the required defining characteristics of situations which are associated with gross behavior. In the laboratory, it is commonplace to speak of *a* stimulus for a given piece of behavior in spite of the fact that the complexities of even relatively simple situations have been widely recognized. However, in considering gross human behavior, one can almost never speak of *a* stimulus. Consider another person as a "stimulus." There are at least two extremely complicated aspects of this person as a "stimulus" for the subject's behavior. First, the actual behavior of the stimulus person has a great number of dimensions of variation each of which may be associated with the observed behavior of the subject. Second, the context in which the stimulus person behaves is never without bearing on the behavior of the subject. Obviously, the simple and complex stimulus situations fall on a continuum. Although we may in later sections use the term "stimulus" as an abbreviation for stimulus situation, the usage should be recognized as such.

In the study of gross human behavior as it occurs in life, the situation designated as a "stimulus" needs to be both practical and plausible. It requires a definition flexible enough so that covariance with diverse phenomena such as catatonic behavior and behavior in a dentist's chair is measurable. A first problem in defining the stimulus situation is to set limits. Of the infinite number of events that might potentially covary with a given piece of behavior, it is necessary to delineate those which we will call the "stimulus." It is not merely a question of selection based on physical description. Additionally, much more than the Gestalt principle of "good figure" needs to be considered. Because a portion of the environment is distinctive, it does not follow that it is the stimulus. Our efforts need to be directed toward identifying stimuli that covary with observed behavior even in the most obscure cases.

In defining the stimulus for gross human behavior as it occurs in life, an extremely complex problem centers around the variation in response by different individuals to the same stimulus. Obviously, this "constant" stimulus must have different characteristics for different responders. No amount of purely physical description of the stimulus will account for the variance in behavior. For example, given a dead older man as the stimulus. Expose two younger men, as subjects, to the stimulus. One responds by casually remarking, "He's dead." The other responds with a violent startle reaction and a cry. The latter is the son of the dead man. Clearly, the past history of the subject is an extremely important characteristic of the stimulus situation. The history of previous responding to the stimulus or an equivalent stimulus accrues to the stimulus as part of its properties, varying from subject to subject. Thus, sheer description of the physical and behavioral characteristics of the stimulus are not enough to account for covariation between stimulus and response.

In studying gross human behavior, definition of the stimulus must include a history of previous experience with the given stimulus, or its equivalent. This requirement involves a complicated process of which we know relatively little. However, there are certain well established principles bearing on the acquisition of behaviors that can help in defining the stimulus situation for our purposes.

The response to a stimulus is some function of the subject's previous behavior in response to a similar stimulus. The more similar the current stimulus to a previously encountered stimulus, the more the subject's behavior will be like that exhibited in response to the earlier stimulus. This is the principle of generalization. It helps us to specify the characteristics of a stimulus that may be related to the observable responses. An example might clarify how the principle helps in the study of gross human behavior. For instance, a subject is observed to display avoidant behavior in response to a man old enough to be his father. Observation of the behavior of the stimulus provides us with data that seem to be unrelated to the subject's response. In other words, the behavior of the older man is not such that avoidant behavior by the subject is reasonable. Knowledge of the similarity of physical appearance of the current stimulus, older man, to the subject's father enables us to describe the stimulus so that the subject's behavior becomes lawful on the basis of generalization. This example is, unfortunately, too simple. Similarity of physical appearance may be an unimportant datum. More important, it seems to us, are the similarity of behaviors exhibited by the current stimulus to those previously displayed by father and the subject's previous responses to father.

Descriptions of the significant aspects of the current stimulus, to which the subject is responding, may be difficult to come by, unless we know of father's behaviors to which the subject previously responded. In terms of the subject's responses, then, these characteristics of the father become characteristics of the current stimulus. By such considerations, we do not mean that the subject is *not* responding to the actually observed behavior of the current stimulus. But we do wish to state that the subject is also reacting to the behavior of the current stimulus related to the previous behavior of father and previous responses of the subject to father. The behavior of the subject in the current situation is some complex function of the actually observable behaviors of the stimulus and those that accrue to the stimulus by virtue of its similarity to father.

Some subjects seem to respond to all older men similarly. They seem unable to discriminate between members of a broad class of stimuli. In such cases, it seems impossible to define the current stimuli in terms of observable behaviors. Thus, a child avoidant of father may exhibit avoidance in the presence of all older men. There are cases in which generalization seems to be maximal and discrimination minimal. A catatonic patient may respond similarly regardless of the classes of stimuli (people) presented to him. In this case, of course, it is obvious that unless the past history of the subject is known it becomes impossible to describe adequately the relevant stimuli.

It seems to us that a working definition of the stimulus for gross human behavior must take into consideration: (1) the physical attributes of the delineated stimulus, e.g., a person, (2) the behavior of this stimulus, (3) the salient features of the environmental context in which the stimulus is presented and (4) the past experience of the subject with the stimulus or its equivalent. In any given situation, these characteristics may vary in weight with respect to their relationship with the observed behavior.

There are a number of issues worth discussing in connection with this position. The first that comes to mind has to do with the accumulation of life experiences of the subject and how these become part of the stimulus, *outside* the subject. This is not an easy message to communicate. The difficulty lies in the insistence on the part of some psychologists that whatever accrues to the subject as a result of life experiences must necessarily be within the subject and thus private knowledge. From our point of view, stimulus-response relationships at the time of occurrence are outside the organism. Since these relationships are always outside the organism, they are always *public* knowledge. Therefore, the past history of the organism is *external* to it, and at any given moment of observation, the characteristics of the eliciting situation are operationally definable. From this behavioristic standpoint, there is not a "private world." This position is the direct antithesis of the phenomenologic approach (Kuenzli, 1959; Combs and Snygg, 1959). The emphasis in our position is on the identifiable, external, eliciting stimulus situation.

The content of verbalizations by people have usually been considered stimuli. In our approach to gross human behavior, the content of verbal behavior by people serving as stimuli is not measured, as such. Thus, the words, "I love you" by a stimulus have no status. Rather, behaviors such as adient movements, displays of affection, helpful behavior, etc. are measured. We do not mean that verbal behavior, itself, is ignored. Thus, frequency of speech, variations in loudness and pitch are characteristics of the stimulus. When these are extreme, such as incessant talking in the presence of the subject, they are data. Specific content may be important in some settings. In our approach, content is considered only in terms of its unusualness and frequency. Thus, consistent *non sequiturs* by the stimulus would, as in the case of other peculiarities of speech, be recorded. Behavior on the part of a stimulus person who, in response to a greeting, consistently responds with an obscenity would be a datum. This position does not deny that people respond to the content of verbal behavior as a stimulus. However, it is our contention that thorough knowledge of the behavioral aspects of communication must precede analysis of content. The properties of verbal content for eliciting behavior cannot be identified without such knowledge.

It is worth mentioning specifically, however much it has been previously implied, that the *response* determines the stimulus. Therefore, for us, stimuli can only be defined in terms of grossly observable human reactions. *There is no other way.* No part of the environment is a stimulus unless it is responded to. This position postulates a stimulus situation outside the organism for every piece of behavior, even when the stimulus situation is difficult to measure and, in some instances, difficult to identify. Thus, the stimulus for what is called "thinking" is often difficult to identify. Nevertheless, our position demands that there be an identifiable stimulus. The direction for the solution to this problem lies in our previously attempted definition of the stimulus situation.

This discussion now leads us directly to consideration of a troublesome problem. This problem centers around such concepts as stimulus constancy, stimulus equivalence and stimulus class. We recognize, of course, that perfect duplication of a stimulus is logically and methodologically impossible in behavioral science. Our solution to this problem stems from two major aspects of our position: (1) our statements concerning the requirements for an adequate definition of the stimulus for gross human behavior and (2) our insistence that stimuli can only be defined in terms of observable responses. An example might clarify our thinking. Although a father's behavior and physical appearance may change from the point of view of an outside observer, a son's responses to father may remain relatively constant throughout life. Therefore, as defined by the son's responses, the stimulus, father, remains constant. In this example, the chief characteristics of the stimulus are determined by the past history of the son. Examples in which the history of the subject have less weight as a defining characteristic of the stimulus are readily available. Thus, a radical change in the physical appearance of father, e.g., loss of both legs, may well produce a change in responding by son. The point we wish to make is that stimulus equivalence is determined by response equivalence. It may seem obvious, but worth mentioning, that the problem of stimulus class is resolved by us by determining response classes.

In our experience, it seems as if the responses of chief concern covary with people as stimuli. The immediate family of a subject is perhaps the most important stimulus. Therefore, we selected as prime stimuli the members of the subject's family, i.e., mother, father, siblings, wife and children. From that beginning, we went to other stimuli consistently in contact with the subject, such as grandparents, peers and other older and younger people. The problem, here, is to get at those aspects of the stimuli which, on *a priori* basis, seem likely to have some bearing on the subject's behavior. Obviously, we don't *know* these parameters. The data are yet to be obtained. Our tentative solution to this problem is to describe the stimuli in detail, always recognizing the fact that when humans observe humans allowance must be made for a large error factor. In order to guide data collection, some framework must be provided. Our choice represents our bias.

Our approach to the problem is to attempt to describe the actual, observable behaviors of the stimuli toward our subject. Attitudes and feelings of the stimuli or about the stimuli are not acceptable data. Our interest lies in descriptions of behavior of the stimulus toward the subject. Perhaps some examples will make our meaning clear. Thus, with siblings as stimuli, we have attempted to define several variables, e.g., Frequency of Contact, Play Activities with the Subject, Restraints on the Subject, Physical Punishment, Displays of Affections, Deviant Behavior and Compatibility of the Stimulus. Each of these variables directs the attention of the Experimenter toward a class of behaviors on the part of the stimulus. Thus, "Displays of Affection" requires that the Experimenter obtain actual incidents of behaviors of this class. These behaviors are defined as patting, stroking, hugging, kissing, etc. We are concerned with such measures as the frequency and amount of these behaviors toward the subject. These data are obtained from the subject, the stimulus and observers of the stimulus-subject relationship, e.g., in the case of siblings, mother, father, other siblings, etc. Data are collected on a particular class of behaviors until the Experimenter establishes consistency of behavior. Similarly with the other variables about Siblings as stimuli. The method of gathering the data and the specific variables for each stimulus are described in a later chapter.

The variables selected for each stimulus on an *a priori* basis are not meant to be final or absolute. Their ultimate status depends on the data to be collected. They are only meant to provide an initial framework for the Experimenter. The estimate of these behaviors must, at present, be crude. However, we can with some degree of certainty state their presence or absence. It seems obvious to us that the variables will be changed, regrouped and redefined as the data emerge. It is important at this stage that as much data as possible about the stimulus be gathered. Undoubtedly, some of the data will have little bearing on the subject's responses. What behaviors of the stimulus are pertinent to the subject's responses are research matters.

REFERENCES

Combs, A. W., and Snygg, D.: Individual Behavior: A Perceptual Approach to Behavior. New York, Harper & Bros., 1959 (rev. ed.).

Guthrie, E. R.: The Psychology of Learning. New York, Harper & Bros., 1935.

Hebb, D. O.: The Organization of Behavior. New York, John Wiley & Sons, Inc., 1949.

Hull, C. L.: Principles of Behavior. New York, Appleton-Century, 1943.

Koffka, K.: Principles of Gestalt Psychology. New York, Harcourt, Brace & Co. Inc., 1935.

Kuenzli, A. E. (Ed.): The Phenomenological Problem. New York, Harper & Bros., 1959.

Lewin, K.: Principles of Topological Psychology. New York, McGraw-Hill, 1936.

Skinner, B. F.: Science and Human Behavior. New York, MacMillan, 1953.

Tolman, E. C.: The Nature and Functioning of Wants. Psychol. Rev. 56: 357-369, 1949.

The Response 4

All observers of living organisms, regardless of their theoretical bias, measure behavior. Observers vary, however, in the nature of the responses studied and the measures applied to these responses. For the human organism, responses range from those only measurable by elaborate electronic equipment to those grossly observable to the naked eye. The response is defined by what the investigator measures and, of course, the nature of his measures. In any given stimulus situation, not *all* responses, nor *all* aspects of any given response, can usually be measured. There is clearly a selective process on the part of the investigator. Take sleeping behavior in a person. One can observe that the person is immobile. One can attach fine measuring instruments to the bed springs. EEG measurements or muscle action potentials can be recorded. Obviously, the measurements taken reflect the bias of the investigator.

We shall now attempt to define what constitutes a response within the framework of gross human behavior. It might be well to begin with some examples. Thus, the growth of cancerous tissue within the organism might, in another frame of reference, be considered a response. Within the framework of gross human behavior, however, such tissue change is not an object of study, per se. What does concern us are the gross behaviors associated with the cancer, such as responses to known stimuli as wife and children. "Anxiety" is usually considered a response. Such a concept has no status from our standpoint. What concerns us are tremor, twitching, flushing, etc., not pulse rate or respiration rate, as measured by the usual instruments. Respiration rate *may* be an object of interest if it is grossly observable in panting behavior. Similarly,

GSR is not of concern to us, but grossly observable perspiration is. The same reasoning applies to "responses" to attitudinal scales and other similar instruments. What we observe in such cases are "paper-marking" behaviors.

Although we have considered verbal behavior as a stimulus it is worthwhile to discuss this problem, briefly, on the response side. The content of a verbal response such as "I hate you" is not the subject matter of the present approach. For such a response, the measures applied are presence or absence, loudness, pitch, etc. Unless grossly observable nonverbal behavior such as avoidance or attacking occurs, these are the only measures used. An example might make our meaning clearer. A gray lady in a mental hospital avows she "loves" the patients. However, when she is observed in contact with the backward patients, she shows avoidant and fearful behavior. Our approach ignores the *content* of her verbalization as such, and studies her behavior in response to the stimuli. Another example might be the case of a small, "Casper Milquetoast" who asks directions to the bathroom of an angry, large man, gets told correctly but cannot find his way to the bathroom. The important characteristic of the behavior in such a case seems to be not the verbalization but, rather, the nonverbal behavior. We do not wish to deny the importance of the content of verbal behavior, but merely to re-emphasize our interest in the basic attributes of verbal behavior such as loudness and its nonverbal concomitants. It seems to us that such an approach is propaedeutic to theorizing in problems of communication.

From this position, responses to questionnaires become for us merely paper-marking responses to a stimulus situation which consists of paper, pencil, examiner, etc. Similarly with all paper and pencil tests. Parenthetically, it might be noted that this position requires that an intelligence test consist of the observation of gross human behavior in response to a stimulus situation as defined by us.

In presenting this systematic approach, objection has frequently been raised that it cannot account for so-called "thinking." Thinking and cerebration are usually considered synonymous. Cerebration is not grossly observable and, therefore, is not an object of study for us. When "thinking" is said to occur it is measurable from our point of view by such behavioral concommitants as pacing, immobility, writing, etc. A mathematician is writing a formula. Thinking may be said to occur in such a situation. For us, writing formulae is a grossly observable response in a stimulus situation. Whether or not the mathematician is "thinking" is outside the scope of our approach. Our efforts are directed toward describing the response and attempting to measure the specific stimulus correlates of such behavior.

Thus far, we have been mostly concerned with responses that are not of interest to our approach. The reason for this behavior on our part is simple: We are not quite sure what we mean by a response within the context of our discussion. There are a few parameters of a response that we feel certain about. For instance, the response should be discriminable with the naked eye. Second, the presence or absence of the response should be agreed upon by independent observers. It seems as if the response ought to be lawful in the sense that it occurs with some consistency in a particular stimulus setting. From here on out we are not quite so certain. Of the almost infinite number of responses that the human organism is capable of, with which ones shall we concern ourselves?

There are two broad types of responses of interest to us. There are those responses in which a consistent covariation can be established between the definable stimulus and the response. Other responses can be observed for which the stimulus is not as readily apparent. The differentiation is on the basis of the relative difficulty in identifying the stimulus. This general distinction corresponds roughly to the differentiation between operant and respondent behavior (Skinner, 1938) or classic and instrumental activity (Hilgard and Marquis, 1940).

The first type of responses are those which are observed to be related to known stimuli. The responses of a child to his mother are of this variety. For example, whenever mother appears, the child moves toward her. If this stimulus-response event occurs with a high frequency, then it is assumed that the observed response, movement toward, is related to the definable stimulus, mother. Although mother is only a part of the total stimulus situation, our focus is on her and the subject's responses to her. As noted previously, the earlier occurrence of the stimulus-response sequence is part of the total current situation. At this juncture, however, we do not wish to complicate the discussion but rather focus on "Responses to Known Stimulus Situations."

The second type of responses are those for which definition of the stimulus is much more difficult and, in many cases in our present state of knowledge, impossible. For working purposes, we term these "Operant Responses" after Skinner (1938). Within our framework, such responses as eating, sleeping and eliminating are operants. It should be kept in mind that this position derives from our definition of the stimulus. For some systematic positions behaviors such as sleeping and eating would not be considered operant responses since the physical characteristics of the stimulus situation can be defined within the organism. Our approach requires that not only the physical attributes of the stimulus situation be defined but also previous experiences with a similar stimulus situation. Additionally, our approach requires that the stimulus be *outside* the organism. Internal events, such as bladder pressure have no status as stimuli in our position. In this case, there are stimulus characteristics such as presence of toilet and elapsed time since last urination that have a bearing on the response, but other characteristics of the current stimulus situation such as past history need to be known before consistent covariation can be established. With sleeping behavior, for instance, it is known that the presence of darkness, elapsed time since last sleep and amount of previous activity vary with the sleeping behavior. However, these characteristics of the total stimulus situation are not consistent predictors of sleeping behavior.

Subjects may have consistent ways of responding to people who are unknown to them. Thus, a subject is introduced to an older woman. His response can be observed and measured. In such a case, the characteristics of the stimulus that are related to the observed response are not readily apparent. It may be that knowledge of previous experience of the subject with a similar stimulus will add to the definition of the stimulus so that the response is lawful, but this is a matter for further study. In the absence of such knowledge we classify these behaviors as "operant."

Within the class of operant responses, there are degrees of identifiability of the stimulus. For instance, what are the stimuli for writing a novel? We can define the total stimulus situation in which the novel writing behavior occurs, but, in our present state of knowledge, we can see no lawful relationship between the definable characteristics of the stimulus situation and the observed behavior. Much more research is required before the stimulus characteristics pertinent to such behavior can be identified.

There are, therefore, two broad classes of responding in gross human behavior that, at this point, concern us. These classes are not dichotomous but continuous, ranging from responses to readily identifiable eliciting stimuli to responses where the eliciting aspects of the stimuli are obscure. For purposes of convenience, we have termed these "Responses to Known Stimuli" and "Operant Responses." Within these broad classes of responding we have designated certain subclasses. Under the class "Responses to Known Stimuli," we have identified subclasses such as responses to Mother, Father, School and Job. Under the class "Operant Responses," we have identified responses such as Eating, Sleeping and responses to unknown people. Further, under the subclasses of responding we have, on an *a priori* basis, attempted to specify variables such as "Adience-Abience," "Cooperativeness" and "Competition." This situation is further complicated by the concept of response equivalence.

Obviously, there are responses that are related in the sense that they have similar effects on the environment. For instance, a subject can pick up a glass of water in many ways. Most of these ways will be equivalent in the sense that the hand is used to bring the water to the subject's mouth. Consider a batter in a baseball game. One batter will hold his bat over his shoulder, another will twitch it back and forth. For our purposes these responses are equivalent if the batter hits the ball with appoximately the same end result. The point we are trying to make is that different kinds of responses accomplish the same environmental change and that, within limits, the nuances of such behaviors are not of concern to us. However, we recognize that such a concept when carried to more complicated behaviors presents problems that we cannot, in ou present state of knowledge, resolve. For instance, there must be a whole class of behaviors which might be labeled "avoidant" with respect to a specific stimulus. The determination of the members of such a response class is a research matter. It can be resolved only by systematic observation.

So far, we have not been very successful in defining a response. There does, however, seem to be one way of looking at responses that makes sense to us. If the response has a differential effect on the environment, we are interested in it. Perhaps a few examples might make our thinking clearer. Thus, a person is observed to tap a desk or stroke a pencil occasionally. If these have no observable effect on the immediate environment, then they are not of interest. Consider a man at a desk with another person in the room. An occasional stroking of the pencil will have no observable effect on the environment. If, on the other hand, our subject continually strokes his pencil, this behavior may elicit from the environment (the other person) a response, a movement, a verbalization, etc. Another subject only occasionally strokes his pencil, but, in addition, he taps his toe on the floor, drums the desk top and scratches his ear, this whole sequence occuring with high frequency and intensity. Now the pencil stroking becomes of interest in the total response pattern which presumably effects the other person. Thus, what response nuances to observe and measure cannot, in our present state of knowledge, be definitely stated. At the moment, it is true, we are primarily interested in the differential effects of the response on people. However, we do not feel bound by this initial attack on the problem. It just seems easier to begin that way.

The behavioral scales which will be discussed in a later section represent a first approximation to measurement in this area. The problem in setting up the scales on an *a priori* basis was one of setting some limits on the amount of detail to be included. The possibilities are almost infinite. Our solution was to select those variables which seem reasonable and grossly descriptive of the subject's behavior. Thus, the responses to the known stimulus situation "Father" include Helpful Behavior, Copying Behavior, Fear Behavior and Displays of Affection. Each of these consist of a number of observable, equivalent responses preselected without data. The variables and the classes of responses which define them will emerge from systematic observation. All we can do at present is make a beginning.

REFERENCES

Hilgard, E. R., and Marquis, D. G.: Conditioning and Learning. New York, Appleton-Century, 1940.
Skinner, B. F.: The Behavior of Organisms. New York, Appleton-Century, 1938.

Basic Observations of Behavior 5

A first consideration in systematically observing behavior is to delimit and label the behavior under observation. This process appears to be simple (although it is not) as in sleeping behavior. In other cases, the delimiting and labeling is admittedly extremely crude as in Restraining Behavior or in Displays of Affection. It should be borne in mind that the purpose of the present systematic approach is to discover and more precisely define pieces of behavior of predictive and heuristic value. Therefore, in dealing with variables such as "Displays of Affection" the delimiting and labeling is arbitrary. The status of this variable (if it is one) depends on the outcome of future research. In spite of these handicaps, the behavior under observation must be defined.

Variables such as Verbal and Physical Punishment for the stimulus, Adience-Abience for the subject's response to a known stimulus and Cleanliness for Operant Responses constitute class labels which encompass a large number of specific behaviors as yet unknown. Although, obviously, many of the behaviors included in the Operant Response Class, "Cleanliness," are known, there remains the question of the behaviors that delimit this response class. For instance, a person is in the water. Is he swimming or washing? A person is lying down, immobile with his eyes closed. Is he sleeping? What responses must be displayed by the subject in order to remove this behavior from the response class "Sleeping?" The answer to these questions lies in the systematic observation of specific behaviors and the situations in which they occur. Until such data are accumulated labeled classes of behavior can only be guides to data-gathering.

Every piece of behavior emitted by an organism has several observable characteristics. Much experience in observing infrahuman behavior has resulted in a number of established measures. Fortunately, these measures are also applicable to human behavior. Whenever possible, all or some of them should be used in describing human behavior. This chapter is concerned with the description of these measures. Data obtained by the use of the measures to be described will provide the specifics of behavioral classes.

The measures to be attempted for all data are as follows:

1.	frequency	6.	amount
2.	latency	7.	variety
3.	rate	8.	conditions
4.	intensity	9.	direction
5.	duration	10.	correctness

The first and probably the most obvious observation to apply to a piece of behavior is its occurrence. Occurrence has *frequency* attached to it, ranging from zero frequency to high frequency within a specified opportunity. Thus, in a laboratory experiment on verbal conditioning, the frequency of occurrence of the conditioned word or class or words can be counted in a given ten minute period. This counting, in the laboratory, can be fairly precise. However, when considering pieces of gross human behavior over a period of several years such precision cannot, in most cases, be obtained. In some cases, the measurement will be relatively easy such as the frequency of Eating behavior, but in other cases, such as Displays of Affection, the estimate will be difficult. The measurement of behaviors subsumed under the variable Displays of Affection, for instance, is further exacerbated by the fact that we do not know precisely the specific behaviors encompassed by this variable. Therefore, each of the specific behaviors which are deemed to constitute this variable need to be observed and their frequency noted.

A measure closely related to the frequency of a response is its *latency*. The piece of behavior under observation begins after a certain time lapse from the presentation of the stimulus. The time elapsing from the presentation of the stimulus to the onset of the behavior is called *latency*. A simple and much used laboratory measure of latency is reaction time. In the gross behavior we are interested in, latency can be applied to most behavior. Thus, S is asked a question. What is the elapsed time from the end of the question to the beginning of his response? In this case, latency can be an important measure differentiating between the quick responding subject and the slow responder. In some behaviors, latency as a measure is difficult to apply or, perhaps, impossible. Thus, for those behaviors where the stimuli are not readily apparent, latency as a measure is less applicable. An example might be visits to a physician for a physical check-up.

The frequency of a response is the number of times it occurs in a given length of time. The *rate* of response refers to a characteristic of single responses. Thus, a response may occur with a frequency of three times a day, such as eating. Regardless of frequency some S's chew rapidly, some slowly. The *rate* measure is meant to differentiate these two. Rate, here, is speed of chewing. Given a constant amount of food, how long does S take to consume it? In some instances, frequency and rate correspond, e.g., frequency and rate of chewing in a given period of time.

In addition to frequency, latency and rate, a response also has an "effort" characteristic, called *intensity*. An example of intensity would be the loudness level with which a person talks. Intensity as a measure might be applied to sleeping behavior. Some S's sleep heavily and are difficult to awaken, others sleep lightly. Some S's put much effort into socializing. Intensity, as measure, can be applied to a variety of behaviors.

We have suggested a number of measures that involve time. We wish, now, to suggest another time measure, an overriding one to be applied to all data, namely, *duration*. Each specific response, and response class, occurs over time. It is important that this time be observed. Thus, "duration" measures the time a person sits in the bath tub each time a bath is taken. This measure is not obtained by frequency, rate, latency or any of the other measures.

In addition to these measures, we have found that certain other measures are required to describe adequately gross behavior. It will be seen that some of the additional measures to be discussed will partially overlap with the basic measures in some instances. In other instances, the additional measures seem to be independent. The first of these additional measures is *amount*. Some behaviors seem to have amount attached to them, e.g., amount of food consumed. It should be borne in mind that this measure cannot be applied to some variables. For instance, the variable, "Illnesses and Accidents," subsumed under the "Health" category would not be amenable to measurement by "Amount"; rather, frequency would apply.

Some response categories have a qualtitative characteristic attached to them which we shall call *variety*. For example, the subject may clean his teeth by brushing, using dental floss, toothpick, fingers or rinsing. Variety, as a measure, is an important guide to systematic observation. It helps us accumulate the specific behaviors for a *class* of behaviors. What are the variety of ways in which son greets mother? What are the variety of ways in which sleeping behavior is exhibited? If the question of variety is not put, the data will not be accumulated.

This notion of variety is, in some cases, similar to another measure we wish to introduce, *conditions*. By "conditions" we mean any unusual and consistent aspects of the stimulus situation associated with the behavior under observation. Thus, the subject listens to symphony music each time he takes a bath. Often the notion of "conditions" will be covered by other variables. This measure should always be applied to the data to insure that they are complete.

Much behavior has directional characteristics. For instance, the subject moves toward or away from a stimulus. Take a subject in an "open field" situation e.g., a social gathering composed of different groups of people. Toward which group does he gravitate? Does he move toward the older age group, female group or peer males? It is difficult to conceive of a description of behavior, in which the subject moves, that does not include the direction of movement. In some cases, in which the subject does not move, as, for instance, in a social situation, the lack of direction is a datum. Therefore, although *direction* may not apply to many behaviors, e.g., chewing, it is a basic measure to be attempted for all behaviors.

One other measure which we think important is less objective than those so far discussed. It might be considered the appropriateness, relevance or *correctness* of the response. In some cases, the correctness of a response can be objectively measured as in the "correct" turn of a rat at a choice point or in "correctness" of response in a complex reaction time experiment. In other cases, however, judgment needs to be applied in order to estimate correctness. Thus, the response to "Good morning" has many *varieties* such as "Hello," "Good morning," and "Hi," but the response to the stimulus "Good morning" of "I am unhappy" seems less correct, occuring in our culture with very low frequency. In the example just given, judgment is clearly involved.

Each of these measures should be applied to all behavior observed, whether it be on the stimulus or subject side. Not all of them will be applicable in every case, but if they are attempted it will insure that significant data are not missed. Examples will make our meaning clearer.

Eating is an operant response. In describing eating behavior, an attempt should be made to apply the ten basic measures as follows:

    1. Frequency—number of times per day eating behavior is exhibited.

    2. Latency—interval between presentation of food and onset of eating behavior.

    3. Rate—speed of chewing behavior.

    4. Intensity—effort put into mastication as assessed by biting of bones, hard bread, etc.

5. Duration—amount of elapsed time from onset of eating behavior to its end, for breakfast, lunch, dinner, snacks, etc.
6. Amount—quantity of food consumed each time the subject eats.
7. Variety—different kinds of food consumed.
8. Conditions—stimulus situations under which food is consumed.
9. Direction—does not seem applicable.
10. Correctness—does he use a knife to eat peas?

Displays of Affection is a gross variable on the stimulus side under which a large number of specific behaviors can be subsumed. In observing behaviors which, on *a priori* basis, might be labeled "Displays of Affection," the basic measures are attempted. Thus, in observing the reaction of the stimulus, "mother," toward the subject the basic observations are made somewhat as follows:

1. Frequency—the number of times the specific behaviors deemed "affectionate" occur. Thus, how often does, for instance, hugging, occur? kissing? stroking? etc.
2. Latency—time elapsing between presentation of the subject to the stimulus, mother, and the onset of affectionate behavior on her part.
3. Rate—does not seem particularly applicable, but may be in some instances as, for instance, speed of patting.
4. Intensity—how vigorously is affection displayed, e.g., the bear-hug.
5. Duration—the span of time over which a specific display of affection occurs.
6. Amount—this measure appears to be estimated by frequency and intensity for the variable "Displays of Affection."
7. Variety—the number of ways affection is displayed.
8. Conditions—characteristics of the stimulus situation under which affection is displayed, e.g., only on leaving or arriving from a journey.
9. Direction—does not seem applicable.
10. Correctness—a judgment has to be made, e.g., is the display of affection appropriate.

It needs to be re-emphasized that we do not know, at the present stage of our research, what constitutes "significant" behavior for the variables, the stimulus situations and the responses. Therefore, it is necessary to obtain as much data as possible.

Interview Techniques 6

Ideally, the behavior of a subject should actually be observed under a variety of stimulus situations. An around-the-clock motion picture with sound would presumably supply the most valid data. Additionally, as mentioned previously, the observer with his camera should be invisible. Such observations should begin with the birth of the subject. Obviously, these conditions cannot be met. We must settle for something less than the ideal. Thus, except for observations made during an interview session, the data are gathered by the interview method. Most of the data are obtained from verbal report of the subject. Other data may be obtained from other informants. We wish, now, to focus on the face-to-face relationship between examiner and informant. This relationship is crucial, since on it depends the validity of the obtained data.

At the outset, it is important for the experimenter to recognize what it is he is demanding of the subject. The subject is required to meet a level of confidence that is far beyond the usual social demands. One can think of confidence in another person at various levels. For instance, some people we trust with a small amount of money. Others we will loan large amounts. We have sufficient confidence in a few people to trust them with our lives. But most of us have no one that we will trust so completely that we will reveal our most intimate behaviors. For instance, how many of us would easily tell another about self-admiration activities while standing naked before a full-length mirror. In obtaining the behaviors in which we are interested, we are essentially asking the subjects to undress themselves psychologically. The confidence required of the subject is not easily come by. *It has to be won.*

Much of what is required to win the confidence of the subject lies in the background of the Examiner. It seems to us that he should have had experience in observing, predicting and modifying gross human behavior (usually called "psychological diagnosis and treatment"). He should, himself, have been a subject of study. During the course of obtaining his background, he should have acquired an acceptance and appreciation of human foibles. He should have sufficient knowledge of human behavior so that from observation of the current behavior he can predict much of the experiential background of the subject. This ability of the Examiner instills confidence in the subject.

It is our opinion that to become an Examiner (in the sense that we are using the term) one should have a background which involves the systematic observation of infrahuman subjects. Ideally, the courses of study should begin with lower order animals and progress up the phylogenetic scale to adult humans. Such study contributes to the Examiner's capacity for uninvolved, objective observation of human behavior. Being human ourselves, we are too prone to respond to verbal behavior to the detriment of observing and recording what the organism is doing. Experience with animals teaches one to avoid the pitfalls of verbal behavior.

The total stimulus situation must be such that the elicitation of verbal reports of behavior is fostered. The place of interview should be completely private and the anonymity of the subject insured by the use of a code number rather than the name of the subject. The qualifications of the Examiner should be such that the subject knows that ethical standards will be observed. A first order business is to reinforce the subject for volunteering many hours of his time. This reinforcing is not only done by expressing gratitude, but also by explaining in detail to the subject's satisfaction the purpose of the series of interviews. With adult normal subjects, we have typically found that they are grateful for the opportunity to look at their environment and their responses to it from the vantage point of a professional person. During this initial contact, the

Examiner must be alert to areas of sensitivity in the subject and attempt to desensitize him in a reassuring manner. For instance, the subject may express the fear that the Examiner may make demands on him that he cannot meet. In such a case, the Examiner needs to reassure the subject such demands will not be made. He needs to let the subject know that the interviews will not be stressful.

This is as good a place as any to discuss some general characteristics of the type of interview we have found that yields the most data. There are certain types of interviews called "stress interviews." In the interviews we advocate the data are yielded, not extracted. The emitting of words by the subject is reinforced. These words are then "shaped" in the direction of behavioral incidents. Cues for eliciting behavioral reports are provided by the Examiner. Thus, in studying the current behavior of a sibling, the subject may be asked, "When was the last time you saw your brother?" Responses about his brother are reinforced in the usual way by interest and verbal acknowledgement. This interest can express itself by inquiring in detail about the time and place and the behavior exhibited by the brother. The point we wish to make is that the process whereby behavioral data are accumulated can, in itself, be reinforcing.

Although the Examiner is accepting, nondemanding and noncritical in his behavior toward the subject, he maintains his role as an investigator. The interview is *not* allowed to become one in counselling. It has been found that subjects will often tend to tell their troubles or to digress. In such cases, the Examiner continues to respond acceptingly, but also in his responses provides cues for the behavior in which he is interested. For instance, a subject, when the topic of his brother is introduced, begins to tell about his feelings and what he thinks are those of his brother. Suppose the subject relates that his brother doesn't "like him." The Examiner responds by inquiring if the brother did anything to give the subject this feeling, finds out time, place and behavior. The feelings expressed by the subject are not behavior, but can be used by the Examiner to shape the subject's responses so that behavior *is* reported. The acceptance of the subject's feelings does not interfere with obtaining reports of behavior. If the Examiner is consistently oriented toward providing cues for the elicitation of behavioral data the interviews will not become counselling sessions. The Examiner's role as an investigator is maintained.

Another characteristic of the interview that mitigates its stressfulness is the order in which topics are introduced. Thus, if the total history of the subject is to be studied, current behavior is investigated before earlier behavior. Within current behavior, certain aspects of operant responding, the responses of known stimuli to the subject and his responses to them are introduced first. With known stimuli, we have typically begun with grandparents, since for most subjects this is a relatively insensitive area. Beginning with relatively insensitive areas such as eating and sleeping allows for a span of time during which the process of reinforcement fosters the building of a habit of verbal responding by the subject. This procedure makes the later eliciting of information in more sensitive areas easier. Thus, a presumably unmarried young female did not reveal the fact that she was secretly married until the end of the tenth interview. Up to that time, no one except her and her husband knew of the marriage. The habit of verbal responding to the Examiner became prepotent over previous habits.

We have experienced relatively little difficulty in obtaining reports about current behavior. However, obtaining data from the early life of the subject presents a problem. If a subject is asked about his early experiences with a stimulus on initial contact, it has been found that the memories will be scattered and refer to a phase of life later than the one of interest. For example, when the subject is asked for an early memory of a parent, he will often respond by relating an incident of his tenth year. Obviously, if we are interested in the first ten years of life, we need behavioral data from as much of the ten years as possible. We have found that this sort of data is more easily obtained after the subject has been cued to responding by reporting on his current behavior. Nevertheless, obtaining data about the very early years of life from the subject remains a problem.

To solve this problem, we would like to suggest two techniques which we have found useful. An obvious first procedure would be to obtain information from collaterals such as parents, siblings, neighbors and friends. This is a time-consuming process which very often involves visiting the scene of the subject's early life. The investigation needs to be continued until the consistency of the behavior of the stimuli encountered by the subject and his responses to them is established. This process also serves the purpose of being a validating cross-check for the data obtained from the subject.

The second technique which we advocate is to be used only as a last resort when other procedures have failed to yield consistent data. We are suggesting, here, the use of deep relaxation and/or hypnosis as an aid in the elicitation of verbal reports of early experiences. From what the Examiner knows about the early experiences of the subject, he sets a stimulus situation and then, with the subject under deep relaxation, asks the subject to respond. This technique is described elsewhere (Pascal, 1947). For instance, a subject in discussing his father reports that his father was a travelling salesman during the first five years of the subject's life. The subject, however, cannot report any behaviors related to father for this phase of his life. The Examiner knows approximately the characteristics of the stimulus situation regarding father which were experienced by the subject during these first five years, e.g., time, place and frequency of contact. Now, he helps the subject to a state of deep relaxation. While the subject is in this condition, the Examiner sets the stimulus situation to which the subject is asked to respond. In the present case, the stimulus situation might be described somewhat as follows:

"Imagine you are four years old. You are little. The table-top seems high. You are at home. Your father has been away and now is coming in the door. What did you do? What did he do? Then what happened?" This procedure seems to elicit data often not obtained in the vis-a-vis situation.

It is obvious that the use of the procedure described above requires that the Examiner be a highly trained person. He needs to know enough about the effects of such a procedure so that his role as an investigator can be maintained. We do not wish to be placed in the position of lightly advocating this procedure. Sometimes, it is not necessary. However, we do feel that when the procedure is used the Examiner should be skilled in hypnosis and related techniques. Care should be exercised that amnesia is not induced. In some fearful subjects, the experiencing of amnesia has a detrimental effect on the later data-gathering. It has been found that the application of deep relaxation may elicit "painful and repressed" memories. The Examiner is warned that in such cases the thin line between investigation and counselling becomes rather indistinct. He must exercise every effort to recover his role as an investigator. He must continue to provide cues for the elicitation of behavioral reports.

This brief discussion of interview techniques is not intended as a substitute for clinical experience. Rather, it is written on the assumption that the investigators who will employ the present approach will come to it with a background in the diagnosis and treatment of behavioral problems. The techniques presented should be considered as an addendum to such a background directed toward (1) obtaining the data required and (2) maintenance of the investigatory role. However, in spite of all precautions, it must be recognized that there will be instances in which the investigatory role cannot be maintained.

It is obvious that in dealing with individuals with known behavioral deviancies ("psychotics," "neurotics") the investigatory role cannot be maintained unless the investigator is collaborating with another professional person who assumes treatment responsibility. We have used many individuals with known deviancies as subjects under such circumstances and have experienced no difficulty in keeping to the investigation. However, we have experienced difficulties with so-called "normal" subjects. It is by dint of such experiences that we have come to first advocate careful screening of "normal" subjects and second, careful adherence to the suggestions contained in this chapter to avoid the investigatory interviews becoming counselling sessions.

REFERENCE

Pascal, G. R.: The use of relaxation in short-term psychotherapy. J. Abnorm. & Social Psychol. 42: 226-242, 1947.

Behavioral Incidents 7

The previous chapter considered some aspects of interview techniques particularly pertinent to our approach. This chapter also bears on interview technique. However, the matter we wish to consider, here, is so crucial to our systematic position that we feel it warrants a separate chapter. So far we have made many references to obtaining verbal reports about actual behaviors but have not specified how these are to be obtained.

The method we have evolved for obtaining information about actual behavior is related to the work of at least three investigators: Murray (1938), Flanagan (1954) and Kinsey (1948). Murray defines an *episode* as "a single creature-environment interaction" [p. 42]. He further states "the biography of a man may be portrayed abstractly as an historic route of themas" [p. 43], the *thema* being defined as "the dynamical structure of a simple *episode*" [p. 42]. For us, Murray's contribution is his focus on small, cumulative units of behavior which may become the variables describing gross human behavior.

Kinsey's problem was similar to ours in that he had to depend on verbal reports of behavior. He writes:

If, in lieu of direct observation and experiment, it is necessary to depend upon verbal report by transmitted records obtained from participants in the activities that are being studied, then it is imperative that one become a master of every scientific device and of all the arts by which any man has ever persuaded any other man into exposing his activities and his innermost thoughts. Failing to win that much from the subject, no statistical accumulation, however large, can adequately portray what the human animal is doing. [p. 35]

Kinsey's actual experiences in accumulating behavioral data have formed one of the important bases of our approach to the problem of obtaining such data from verbal reports.

Flanagan's approach is similar to Murray's in many respects. However, Flanagan has been primarily concerned with the significance of pieces of behavior for predetermined criteria, the criteria ultimately being defined by the collected samples of behavior.

The critical incident technique outlines procedures for collecting observed incidents having special significance and meeting systematically defined criteria. By an incident is meant any observable human activity that is sufficiently complete in itself to permit inferences and predictions to be made about the person performing the act. To be critical, an incident must occur in a situation where the purpose or intent of the act seems *fairly clear* to the observer and where its consequences are *sufficiently definite* to leave little doubt concerning its effects. [1954, p. 327, italics ours]

From these three sources we have conceived of an episode of behavior which we have called the *Behavioral Incident* (BI). As a construct it is similar to both Murray's *episode* and Flanagan's *critical incident*. It is similar to Kinsey in the method of gathering the data. A BI is an interaction between a subject and a stimulus. The duration of the incident depends on the activities of the stimulus and subject. As long as the behavior of the subject in the stimulus situation remains relatively constant, the BI continues. Obviously, the phrase "relatively constant" is a judgmental matter. We feel, like Flanagan, that the change in behavior terminating a BI should be "fairly clear" and "sufficiently definite" to the observer. Thus, if two people are talking and one leaves the room, that particular BI is over. If, on the other hand, the two people are talking and a child enters the room whether or not the same BI continues or a new one begins depends on the degree of behavioral change in the two people in response to what might be considered a new stimulus situation. If the behavior of the two people does not change, the stimulus situation has not changed. But, if the behavior of the two people changes so that now they begin to talk to and fondle the child a new BI begins in response to what is now a different stimulus situation. The point, here, is that the BI terminates when there is a radical change in the stimulus situation, but the only way

we can know about this change is from the behavior of the
respondents. We can, now, make a more definitive statement
about what we mean by a BI. *A BI is a stimulus-response
sequence in gross human behavior which endures so long as
there is no radical change in the stimulus situation as defined
by the responses of the subject to it.*

BIs are not easy to come by. Most interviewees tend to
give interpretive statements rather than descriptions of behavior. In addition, we have found that the Examiner, himself, is apt to accept these interpretive statements. For instance, the subject says "I played a lot with my father when
I was young." *This is not a report of behavior.* It just seems
like one. In such a case, the Examiner should inquire about
the first time that the subject remembers playing with his
father. Then, he should establish a given occasion. There-
upon, he questions the subject concerning the specific behavior
of father and his responses to him. The questioning proceeds
somewhat as follows: "Where were you? What was the first
thing you remember that father did? Then what did you do?
Then what did he do?" The questioning continues until the
actual behaviors of father and the subject's responses to them
are described. Thereafter, the subject is asked for further
incidents of play with father. Enough such incidents are
obtained until the consistency of the behaviors of father and
son are established.

Little Johnny is on the porch playing when father comes
home from work. Father is coming up the walk. Johnny runs
toward him. Father ignores him and continues on into the
house. This is a BI. If father bends over, picks up Johnny
and hugs him, saying "Hi, son," this begins another BI. Johnny
says, "Hi, Daddy," and at the same time hugs him around
the neck. Father lowers Johnny to the walk. Then, taking
him by the hand, father leads the way into the house. He goes
to the kitchen and releases Johnny's hand and embraces his
wife. Johnny leaves the room. The greeting BI between
Johnny and father is, at this point, terminated. If Johnny,
while mother and father are embracing, attempts to get be-

tween them this behavior may be the beginning of another BI involving a different sort of activity in a different stimulus situation.

Prolonged contact of our subject with another person may involve a number of BIs, depending on the activities and the stimulus situations. For instance, we are interested in the operant responses of a twenty year old male subject to peer females (not responses to known females). We may ask the subject how he gets along with girls, generally. He says, "Fine." We then inquire about the last blind date he had. He fixes it in time and place for us. The activities were, grossly, greeting, dinner, a dance, driving and parking. The greeting behavior of the subject toward the girl previously unknown to him would constitute a BI. His behavior at dinner toward her, e.g., pulling out the chair for her to sit at the table and helping her with her coat would constitute another incident, behavior while dancing, another, behavior while parking, another, etc. The point is that different activities and different stimulus situations determine the number of BIs.

It is extremely important to obtain enough BIs so that two judges will agree on the nature of the behavior under observation. For instance, we are interested in displays of affection on the part of father toward his son during the first ten years of the son's life. We inquire of the son (our subject) about his early memories of father. We establish a particular memory and proceed as previously described to obtain the actual behavior of the father toward the son in the particular memory. In the subject's account of father's behavior, we look for, and inquire concerning, physical displays of affection from father such as hugging, kissing, patting and stroking. If possible, additional memories described in the same manner are elicited from the subject. For this example, particular attention is paid to physical displays of affection by father in each BI. When enough BIs have been accumulated to establish the consistency or inconsistency of displays of affection, no further data are accumulated from the subject for the particular behavior. BIs are then obtained from the mother, sibling or other relative who had knowledge of father's contacts with our subject during the first ten years of life for the behavior of interest, in this case Displays of Affection. Enough BIs are collected so that, in the opinion of the Examiner, two independent judges will agree on characteristics of the behavior such as frequency, intensity and nature of the activities. The reader should be reminded that behavior can be consistently inconsistent. In some cases, therefore, enough BIs need to be gathered to establish the inconsistency of the behavior of interest. Usually, such a case will require more incidents than those cases in which the behavior of interest is consistent.

We remind the reader that our interest lies in *behavior*. We are not interested in the attitudes or opinions of the subject or others from whom information is obtained. For instance, a subject is asked concerning his mother. He responds that she loves him. We then ask when was the last time he saw her. He responds that it was six months ago. We ask then "what happened?" He replies that she was sweeping the back porch. He said, "Hello." She responded in kind and continued sweeping. Thereafter, the subject reported that he sat on the front porch and read a newspaper. After a half hour during which she continued sweeping and he read the newspaper, he said "Goodbye" and left. Further inquiry revealed that although she lived only one city block from him he saw her, on the average, only once every six months. This latter datum is consistent with the first BI reported. The point we wish to make is that the opinion of the subject sometimes bears little relationship to the actual behavior in which we are interested. The observer must insist on reports of actual behavior and not be misled by opinions or attitudes. Everybody loves his mother, but the concept of love has no status until behaviorally defined.

There is an important point to be made here. The subject is not asked questions that may lead to the expression of opinions or attitudes. The subject is not asked whether he loves his mother but, rather, asked when did he see her last and what happened. If the early relationship with mother is the object of study, then the subject is asked not how did they get along but, rather, what is his first memory of her and the specifics of the occasion.

We recommend that a recording instrument be used in interviewing. When an instrument is not available or feasible (as, for instance, in interviewing a relative at home) the Examiner should make copious notes and immediately after the interview dictate these into a recording machine. We have found, in the latter procedure, that the Examiner, himself, makes interpretive statements. For example, the Examiner may actually obtain the BIs, but report "father played with son consistently." It should be borne in mind that for a reliability study the reports of actual behavior are needed. The Examiner needs to be a faithful recorder, lest the data be biased by his opinions and interpretations. At this stage of the development of the systematic observation of gross human behavior, it is essential that as much data as possible be accumulated.

The use of the BI has been found to be an extremely valuable aid in clinical interviewing. The obtaining of BIs becomes particularly important in those cases where it is felt that the interviewee is not revealing his experiences. Many students of clinical interviewing report statements of the interviewee that are essentially fictitious. For instance, a person known to exhibit "paranoid" behavior is interviewed by a student in the usual clinical manner. The data obtained by the student indicate this person to be "happy and carefree." The BI technique contributes to the obtaining of valid data from the clinical interview. It is difficult to maintain a subterfuge in response to the request for a number of BIs.

Much experience in attempting to collect BIs and in teaching this technique leads to the conclusion that although the BI is simple in conception, the actual process of obtaining BIs is difficult. There is a tendency for the Examiner to settle for accounts of behavior rather than actual incidents. Thus, a subject is questioned concerning his early relationships with siblings. He may, for instance, report playing with them every day after school, even naming specific games. He may then go on to describe the behavior of specific siblings as he remembers it. Although his report may contain a full account of the behaviors of his siblings and his reactions to them, no BIs are given. It is within this context that the Examiner seeks BIs. The difficulty we have encountered is that many examiners tend to stop at this point. What is needed is a specific stimulus-response sequence fixed in time, with as complete a description of the total stimulus situation as can be recalled and the subject's reaction to it. The subject is asked to remember one time when, for instance, he and his younger brother were together as children. He is asked to describe the total situation, the behavior of his brother and his own reactions in detail. Thereafter, other specific memories about his younger brother are sought. This is a time-consuming process, requiring much patience. The Examiner should recognize that much patience is also required on the part of the subject and that any pressure exerted on the subject tends to interfere with the flow of BIs. The setting for the elicitation of BIs needs to be a relaxed one. In some instances, BIs may not be forthcoming, and it may be necessary to return to the topic of investigation at a later time. In other instances, regardless of the efforts of the Examiner, no BIs can be obtained. This fact should be reported.

REFERENCES

Flanagan, J. C.: The critical incident technique. Psychol. Bull. *51:* 327-358, 1954.

Kinsey, A. C. et al.: Sexual Behavior in the Human Male. Philadelphia, Saunders, 1948.

Murray, H. A. et al.: Explorations in Personality. New York, Oxford Univ. Press, 1938.

Stimulus Categories 8

Thus far, we have been concerned with the presentation of a systematic position and general principles applicable to our approach. The three previous chapters have dealt with ways of data-gathering. We are now confronted with the task of *what* data are to be obtained. Our approach to this problem has already been presented. We are interested in molar behavior in response to life situations. If we are asked what particular behaviors we are interested in, we must reply "all of them." Obviously, some investigators such as Kinsey (1948) may be interested in particular behaviors. Others, such as psychoanalysts, may be interested in parent-child relationships. Although our interest lies in the whole range of behaviors, we have attempted to construct an outline for data-gathering which will also satisfy the needs of such investigators. The guide for what data are to be gathered is presented in three basic "Scales" as follows:

SCALE A. STIMULUS CATEGORIES.
I. Known Organisms as Stimuli (Parents, etc.)
  a. Variables (Frequency of Contact, Play Activities, etc.)
    1. Basic Measures (intensity, duration, etc.)
II. Other Known Stimulus Categories (School, etc.)
  a. Variables (Prestige, Social Demands, etc.)
    1. Basic Measures
      SCALE B. RESPONSES TO KNOWN STIMULUS CATEGORIES
I. Responses of Subject to the Variables of Known Stimulus Categories
  a. Basic Measures
II. Other Responses to Known Stimulus Categories
  a. Variables (Adience-abience, Helpful behavior, etc.)
    1. Basic Measures
        SCALE C. OPERANT RESPONSES
  a. Response Classes (Oral Habits, Sleeping, etc.)
    1. Basic Measures

This and the next two chapters will present the Pascal-Jenkins (P-J) Behavioral Scales. (A complete outline of these Scales will be found in the Appendix.) These Scales specify the gross behavioral variables which serve as guide lines for data-gathering. Obviously, the variables were selected on an *a priori* basis and reflect our bias. What variables will eventually emerge lies in the future. For that reason it is important that the guides to data-gathering, the P-J Scales, be not considered limiting but, rather, suggestive. For instance, we have named a variable describing the behavior of a known person as a stimulus, "Compatibility." What specific behaviors define this variable are unknown to us. All we can do is to suggest a large class of possibly related behaviors as a guide to interviewing. We assume the collected stimulus-response relationships (BIs) guided by the Scales will result in an operational definition.

The remainder of the chapter will be ordered as follows. First, we shall consider known organisms as stimuli. Classes of people, such as grandparents, are considered as stimulus categories. For each person, as a stimulus, a number of variables are defined. For each of these defined variables, the basic measures should be applied. For instance, for the stimulus, "Mother," one variable is "Displays of Affection." The basic measures applicable to this variable are Frequency, Intensity, Conditions, etc., in other words, all the measures described in Chapter 5. The reader is reminded that in this chapter we are considering the responses of the stimulus under observation. The stimuli are coded as follows:

"S" indicates a stimulus.

The first number indicates the stimulus category, e.g., S1 stands for "grandparents."

The first number after the decimal point indicates the member of the stimulus category, e.g., S1.4 "Maternal Grandfather."

The number after the "dash" indicates the variable, e.g., S1.4-6 is "Physical Punishment" by Maternal Grandfather.

Following presentation of known people as stimuli, we shall discuss variables to be applied to these stimuli. Thereafter, we present Other Known Stimulus Categories and their variables.

SCALE A. STIMULUS CATEGORIES

I. Known Organisms as Stimuli (S).

S1.1 Paternal grandmother
S1.2 Paternal grandfather
S1.3 Maternal grandmother
S1.4 Maternal grandfather
S2.1 Mother
S2:2 Father
S2.3 Additional parents
S3.1 Oldest sib
S3.2 Next oldest sib, etc.
S4.1 First peer, same sex
S4.2 Second peer, same sex, etc.
S5.1 First peer, opposite sex
S5.2 Second peer, opposite sex, etc.
S6.1 First older person, same sex
S6.2 Second older person,
     same sex, etc.

S7.1 First older person,
     opposite sex
S7.2 Second older person,
     opposite sex, etc.
S8.1 First younger person,
     same sex
S8.2 Second younger person,
     same sex, etc.
S9.1 First younger person,
     opposite sex
S9.2 Second younger person,
     opposite sex, etc.
S10.1 First spouse
S10.2 Second spouse, etc.
S11.1 Oldest child
S11.2 Next oldest child, etc.
S12.1 First animal
S12.2 Second animal, etc.

Variables for Known Organisms as Stimuli

(The variables apply to each of the above stimulus categories. For each variable the basic measures are to be attempted.)

1. Frequency of Contact
2. Play Activities
3. Displays of Affection
4. Providing Behavior
5. Restraints
6. Physical Punishment
7. Verbal Punishment
8. Intellectual Behavior
9. Status

10. Social Behavior
11. Religious Behavior
12. Physical Health
13. Compatible Behavior
14. Role Behavior
15. Variability of Habitat
16. Sexual Behavior
17. Deviant Behavior

II. Other Known Stimulus Categories.

S13.1 First school
S13.2 Second school, etc.
S14.1 First job
S14.2 Second job, etc.
S15.1 First subculture
S15.2 Second subculture, etc.

S16.1 First physical environment
S16.2 Second physical
      environment, etc.
S17.1 First unavoidable illness
      or accident
S17.2 Second unavoidable illness
      or accident, etc.

Variables for Other Known Stimulus Categories

18. Prestige
19. Social Demands
20. Intellectual Demands
21. Physical Demands

22. Religious Demands
23. Financial Demands
24. Restrictiveness
25. Danger

We shall now consider each variable in an attempt at behavioral definitions to guide the interviewer in obtaining data. We reiterate that these variables are only suggestive. Behaviors other than those subsumed under these variables will undoubtedly emerge. They need to be recorded so that the Scales can become better guides. Our attempt to define the variables cannot be exhaustive or definitive. It is our belief that the attempted definitions had better be brief and suggestive lest we run counter to the subjective aspects of word definitions, e.g., "Compatibility" means different behaviors for different investigators.

1. *Frequency of Contact.* How often did the stimulus have contact with the subject during the period under observation? Once a day, week, month? Was the stimulus dead or absent during the period under observation? The intent, here, is to get an estimate of the availability of the stimulus as a basis for gathering data on the other variables. For instance, what did mother or father do during the period of the subject's life under study? Obviously, if father was a travelling salesman or mother worked all day, their availability was limited. Data are obtained in order to estimate the duration and frequency of exposures of the stimulus to the subject.

2. *Play Activities.* When the stimulus was in contact with the subject, what kinds of behaviors were initiated by the stimulus? E obtains BIs concerning the activities of the stimulus. Did the grandfather take the subject to the circus? Did father play "catch" with the subject? With what frequency did these behaviors occur? What variety of behavior occurred? Under what conditions did these behaviors occur? What was their duration? It has been found that questions like the following are helpful in eliciting BIs. If, for instance, the period under investigation is the early life of the subject, "What is

your earliest memory of father (or any other stimulus)? What was he doing? What were you doing? Where were you? How old were you? What happened? What is another early memory of father?" Such questions will, of course, elicit BIs about other variables which should be accepted, but E should pursue BIs about play activities until consistent behavior on the part of the stimulus is established.

3. *Displays of Affection.* This variable has to do with manifest, physical displays of affection by the stimulus toward the subject such as patting, stroking, hugging and kissing. What was the frequency, intensity, amount, variety and conditions of such behavior? BIs are also obtained concerning verbal displays of affection such as terms of endearment, other verbal expressions of affection and such behaviors as gift-giving. A good way to introduce this variable is to query the subject about greeting behavior on last contact or after absence. For instance, what did the stimulus do on seeing the subject as a small child coming home from school?

4. *Providing Behavior.* The purpose of this variable is to guide the interviewer in obtaining data about the behavior of the stimulus which might be termed "nurturant" such as feeding, clothing, housing and generally protective of the subject. Were the physical needs of the subject met by behavior on the part of the stimulus? Use the basic measures that apply. If the early years of life are under investigation, did the stimulus earn as much as his peers? Was the subject clothed as well as *his* peers? What kind of a house did they live in? What was the heating system? The plumbing? What happened when the subject was ill?

5. *Restraints.* This variable has to do with the control exercised by the stimulus over the subject. Were the subject's activities directed by the stimulus? For instance, does the parent decide with whom the subject, as a child, will play, and what games? Does wife determine how many "free" evenings husband shall have? E obtains BIs about controlling behavior by the stimulus directed toward the subject. What is the spontaneity of behavior by the subject in the presence

of the stimulus? For instance, is the small boy (subject) quiet and subdued around father (stimulus), but not when in mother's presence? Does daughter (subject) always check with mother (stimulus) before she accepts an invitation from a young man? What is the frequency, intensity, duration, etc., of such behaviors?

6. *Physical Punishment.* How frequently was the subject actually hit by the stimulus? What variety of physical punishment was used, e.g., hand, stick, foot, etc.? BIs should be obtained showing the conditions, intensity and duration of physical punishment.

7. *Verbal Punishment.* With what frequency was the subject berated, scolded, criticised or, in other words, verbally castigated? Use the basic measures that apply.

8. *Intellectual Behavior.* With what frequency does the stimulus participate in intellectual activities such as reading, attending drama, art shows, lectures? It should be noted that in this variable we are interested in behavior by the stimulus other than that exhibited directly toward the subject. It is assumed, here, that the subject will, in his contact with the stimulus, be exposed to such intellectual activities.

9. *Status.* What is the standing of the stimulus in the subculture in which he lives? This variable, with respect to occupation, generally follows the classification of unskilled, semi-skilled, skilled and professional levels. However, data are also obtained concerning community activities, e.g., United Fund Chairman, Scoutmaster, etc. What behaviors does the stimulus exhibit which can be ordinarily classified as satisfying "prestige needs?"

10. *Social Behavior.* E inquires concerning the activities of the stimulus with people outside the family. What is the frequency, variety, duration and conditions under which the stimulus engages in activities with other people?

11. *Religious Behavior.* This item refers to the frequency of church attendance and/or the amount and frequency of religious practices and ritual in the home. Inquiry is directed

toward the variety and intensity of participation in religious activities by the stimulus.

12. *Physical Health.* What is the frequency of incapacitating physical illness? Its duration, variety, intensity? Data are obtained concerning the physical well-being of the stimulus.

13. *Compatible Behavior.* This variable has to do with the compatibility of the stimulus with people other than the subject, e.g., peers, siblings, parents and spouse. For instance, what is the frequency and intensity of verbal or physical quarrels between the stimulus and such people? To what extent are other people adient toward the stimulus? What are needed, here, is not merely a frequency count of the number of contacts with other people but, rather, BIs indicating the specifics of the behavioral interactions between the stimulus and other people.

14. *Role Behavior.* This variable overlaps with *Social Behavior* and *Play Activities* but is inserted to be sure that E obtains data about behaviors which have to do with the "appropriateness" of the stimulus' behavior for his age, sex and subculture. If the stimulus is a 12 year old boy does he play baseball and football or does he play with dolls? Does a 60 year old woman indulge in activities similar to those exhibited by much younger females? BIs are collected illustrative of typically masculine or feminine behavior.

15. *Variability of Habitat.* This variable has to do with the frequency with which the stimulus moves from one home to another. Obtain data about the frequency and conditions under which habitat is changed.

16. *Sexual Behavior.* What is the actual sexual behavior of the stimulus? Inquiry is made concerning auto-eroticism, homosexual and heterosexual behaviors.

17. *Deviant Behavior.* This item is inserted so that E will obtain data about possible mental illness or behaviors related to it such as hypochondriasis, drug addiction, alcoholism and other pecularities of behavior. Undoubtedly, some of these

behaviors will be uncovered in the course of obtaining data for the other variables, but it is felt that deviant behavior as such warrants a separate variable in order to insure that the data are obtained. (Include mental deficiency.)

It should be noted that not all of the variables have to do with direct contact between stimulus and subject. Some of the variables are behaviors to which the subject may not be directly exposed. Thus, compatible behavior between an uncle (as stimulus) and his spouse may be behavior to which the subject is not exposed and may or may not have any bearing on the subject's behavior. If, however, the stimulus is a parent, such behavior is presumed to have an effect on the subject's behavior. In general, the assumption is made that the more frequent the contact and the closer the relationship the more the characteristics of the stimulus have an impact on the subject's behavior.

The foregoing section has dealt with people as stimuli. We shall now consider Part II of Scale A, Other Known Stimulus Categories. Whereas in Part I of Scale A the stimulus categories need no definition, the categories of Part II require some specification.

S13. School. Attendance at a school is here considered to be a stimulus category. Its characteristics are assumed to have a bearing on the subject's behavior. School, here, is defined as any formal situation which is primarily concerned with teaching the subject intellectual, vocational, artistic or physical skills. Although the major focus in this stimulus category is on formal intellectual schooling, data should also be obtained about other types of schooling such as music, art, dancing, swimming, etc.

S14. Work. Work is defined as any occupational activity for which the subject receives renumeration.

S15. Subculture. We really do not know what a subculture is, systematically speaking. For working purposes, however, we define a subculture as those aspects of the environment, human and nonhuman, which influence the subject's behavior by virtue of his association with them, over and above the specific stimuli in our Scales.

S16. Physical Environment. The intent, here, is to get at those aspects of the geographical environment which may have some bearing on the subject's behavior, e.g., extreme heat or cold, minimal availability of food and the like.

S17. Unavoidable Illnesses and Accidents. In every environment, there exist opportunities for the subject to be exposed to traumatic events over which he has no control. Thus, a child may be brought up in an environment in which pathogenic organisms are prevalent, e.g., malaria. An earthquake or a tidal wave is an environmental event which can have much effect on the subject's behavior and fits our definition of a stimulus. This stimulus category should not be confused with OR6.2 Illnesses and Accidents, an operant response which includes "accident proneness."

We shall attempt to define some variables which apply to these five stimulus categories. These eight variables should be considered for each stimulus category. Some of the variables will be more directly applicable than others. Thus, the variable, Religious Demands, does not seem very appropriate to the stimulus category, Unavoidable Illnesses and Accidents. With a subject who is a member of the Christian Science Church the variable, Religious Demands, may well be an important one in an unavoidable illness or accident. The reader is reminded, again, that the basic measures are to be attempted for each variable.

18. Prestige. The definition of the prestige of a stimulus category is particular to the category. For School, the prestige value is usually determined by a national academic rating, it's reputation, e.g., socio-economic class of its students. For Work, Subculture and Physical Environment the usual socio-economic standards apply. Unavoidable Illnesses and Accidents also may have prestige value, e.g., a broken arm during the ski season, the "fashionable illness." Although we have insisted that BIs be collected for the behaviors subsumed under each variable, we realize that this variable does not lend itself to BIs. Prestige is an intangible but, descriptive character- istic of the environment already established at the time of inquiry.

19. *Social Demands.* This variable has to do with the char- acteristics of the School, Work, Subculture and Physical En- vironment as they effect the subject with respect to the amount of social pressure that is put on him to participate in activities of a social nature whether these be parties, organizational or community activities. How many functions of a social nature is the subject called on to attend by virtue of belonging to these stimulus categories? This variable may not seem to apply to Unavoidable Illnesses and Accidents, yet there are circumstances in which it might be appropriate. Thus, certain communicable illnesses require isolation. Social pressure some- times demands that an athlete with an injury continue to participate. The reader is reminded that we are not, here, interested in the subject's responses but, rather, the social characteristics of the stimulus category. BIs should be collected which pertain to the social demands of the stimulus category.

20. *Intellectual Demands.* With what frequency, intensity, duration, etc., do these stimulus categories require the subject's participation in intellectual activities such as reading, attend- ing plays, art shows, lectures, discussion groups and similar behaviors? This variable is on a continuum from very little to very much. Thus, a person in an igloo near the North Pole may be living in an environment that makes very little in- tellectual demands on him. The point we wish to make is that the absence or near absence of stimulation subsumed under the variable is also datum.

21. *Physical Demands.* What are the physical demands in- herent in the stimulus category? Some schools, for instance, emphasize participation in athletics. Some illnesses, such as tuberculosis, require also complete physical immobilization. Each of the stimulus categories makes some physical de- mands on the subject varying in frequency, intensity, dura- tion and the other basic measures.

22. *Religious Demands.* How much is required from the subject in the way of religious activity by the stimulus category? This variable does not seem to apply to the Physical Environment.

23. *Financial Demands.* To what extent is the subject called on to spend money (or its substitute) as a function of the stimulus categories?

24. *Restrictiveness.* How much freedom of action does the stimulus allow? For instance, in some military schools rigid rules with respect to conduct are enforced by punitive measures. An assembly-line worker is certainly restricted, particularly as contrasted with a college professor. Is the Physical Environment restrictive in the sense of having extremes of climate and geography? Does the Subculture impose rigid rules of conduct on the individual? To what extent is the subject's behavior determined by the stimuli?

25. *Danger.* What is the threat to life as a characteristic of the stimulus? The work of a steeplejack is dangerous, whereas that of a bank clerk is usually considered safe. Data must be gathered about the stimulus which bear on the opportunities for danger afforded by it. What threat to life is inherent in the physical environment such as frequency or intensity of earthquakes, floods, droughts and dangerous animals? With the stimulus category "Unavoidable Illnesses and Accidents" what is the severity of the illness or accident in terms of death rate attributable to it?

There are, in all, 17 stimulus categories and 25 variables. In addition, there are the ten basic measures that should be attempted for each variable. For the ordinary young subject with parents and grandparents living and with at least two sibs, the number of different headings under which data are gathered amounts to something over 2,000 for just the stimulus side. These headings should be considered only as guides to data-gathering. In spite of the large number specified, it may well be that important behaviors have been overlooked.

In our experience, it has been found that very often untrained examiners will begin describing the behaviors of the stimuli without any orienting information about the stimulus. Thus, behaviors indicative of Frequency of Contact and Displays of Affection by grandfather are presented without any description of him. Such a presentation is very often confusing and misleading. It is necessary before beginning a behavioral description of a person as a stimulus to obtain and cite the following information:

Age	Vocation—avocation
Sex	Education
Physical description	Marital status—children
Race—religion	Socio-economic status

For other known stimuli such as School and Physical Environment, a thorough identifying description is required to clarify the data.

REFERENCE

Kinsey, A. C. et al.: Sexual Behavior in the Human Male. Philadelphia, Saunders, 1948.

Responses to Known Stimulus Categories 9

In this chapter we will present Scale B, Responses to Known Stimulus Categories. In the previous chapter, we considered the known stimulus situations to which the subject is exposed. We shall now deal with the subject's responses to these known stimulus situations. This is as good a place as any to admit that we cannot specify, prior to research, what these responses are. However, based on the experiences of many people, and our own, we are prepared to offer a suggestive interview guide for data-gathering. This guide, on the response side, is organized into two broad classes, the responses to the behaviors of the stimuli discussed in the previous chapter and other responses to these known stimuli.

We designate the responses of the subject to the specified behaviors of the stimulus as S-R behaviors. In collecting BIs about the variables on the stimulus side, the Examiner necessarily obtains data about the subject's reactions to the behavior of the stimulus. Thus, in getting BIs about Displays of Affection by, for instance, Father, the Examiner obtains the subject's responses to displays of affection by father. These responses and all the responses to the variables on the stimulus side are what we term "S-R" behaviors. For coding purposes S-R indicates these behaviors and the numbers following this designation correspond to those of the known stimulus categories. For example, S-R1.1-1 refers to responses by the subject to Frequency of Contact on the part of the Paternal Grandmother, and S-R1.1-2 refers to responses by the subject to Play Activities initiated by the Paternal Grandmother.

Over and above the subject's responses to behaviors initiated by the stimulus there remain behaviors initiated by the subject toward known organisms as stimuli. The number of

61

possible responses are, of course, almost infinite. We have arbitrarily decided on 14 as a basis for data gathering. These are listed below. For coding purposes they are preceded by "R-S," "S" and its appropriate code number indicating the stimulus to which the response is made. Thus, R-S1.1-1 is Adience-Abience as a response to Paternal Grandmother.

1. Adience-Abience	8. Competitive Behavior
2. Displays of Affection	9. Physical Aggression
3. Helpful Behavior	10. Verbal Aggression
4. Companionship Activity	11. Restraints
5. Providing Behavior	12. Sexual Behavior
6. Copying Behavior	13. Fear Behavior
7. Dependent Behavior	14. Deviant Behavior

1. Adience-Abience. This is an approach-avoidance variable. When in contact does the subject move toward or away from the stimulus? In the presence of the stimulus does the subject talk to him, or avoid talking to him? This is essentially a directional variable but some of the other basic measures also apply, e.g., conditions, variety, intensity and frequency.

2. Displays of Affection. This variable has to do with manifest physical displays of affection such as patting, stroking, hugging and kissing, initiated by the subject toward the stimulus. BIs are also obtained concerning verbal displays of affection, invitations to social gatherings, gift-giving, etc.

3. Helpful Behavior. This is behavior initiated by the subject toward a known stimulus, behavior which is directed at assisting or facilitating achievement of a goal by the stimulus. For instance, a mother is washing dishes or engaging in some other household task; does the daughter *initiate* cooperative behavior? A parent is in dire financial circumstances; does the adult offspring voluntarily offer aid? Does the subject volunteer assistance to known stimuli in difficulties without a direct request from them? A point we wish to make is that behavior is not particularly "helpful" when it is displayed in response to a direct request or command, or in other circumstances so that refusal may result in some sort of reprisal, however subtle this reprisal may be. On the other hand, a subject cannot offer helpful behavior without knowledge of the need expressed or exhibited by the known stimulus. Whether or not the helpful behavior actually results in direct benefit to the stimulus is beside the point. Thus, a five year old, in attempting to help his father wash the family car, may actually be a hindrance, but he is displaying helpful behavior. The basic measures should, of course, be applied.

4. *Companionship Activity.* This variable has to do with the seeking behavior of the *subject* toward the known stimulus for the purpose of "doing things" together. Given a particular known stimulus, how much effort does the subject put into seeking him out just to spend time with him? What are the variety and conditions of such behavior toward the particular known stimulus? What is the nature of the activities initiated by the subject? The intent, here, is to get at play and social activities initiated by the subject toward a known stimulus, i.e., activities other than vocational or sexual.

5. *Providing Behavior.* This variable deals with the extent to which the subject is concerned with the physical needs of the stimulus for food, clothing, shelter, medical care and safety from danger. Does our subject, an older brother, respond to an attack on a younger brother by protecting him? With what frequency, under what conditions, etc., does the subject exhibit "nurturant" behavior toward the stimulus? This variable parallels the providing variable on the stimulus side but is, of course, concerned with behavior initiated by the subject toward the known stimulus. Thus, a father exhibits providing behavior toward a son. Does the son, in turn, provide for and protect the father?

6. *Copying Behavior.* To what extent is the subject's behavior modeled after that of some known stimulus? Examples are mannerisms of speech and movement, dress and car-driving behavior. To acquire these data, the behavior of the stimulus must be known in specific situations. Inquiry is then directed toward the subject's behavior in similar stimulus situations.

How much is the behavior of the child like that of his father? To what extent is the behavior of our subject similar to that of an "admired" friend?

7. *Dependent Behavior.* This is a variable with many clinical overtones. It seems to us to lead to an important area of inquiry, but we are not sure what it means in behavioral terms. However, we will suggest several questions which should be fruitful in obtaining data of interest. To what extent does the subject seek out a known stimulus prior to reacting to an environmental situation? Does the child "cling" to his "mother's apron strings?" What is the subject's "freedom of action" in the sense that he can act on his own initiative? BIs are collected about events requiring a decision by the subject, e.g., changing jobs. Does a 12 year old child always ask permission of his parents before leaving the house? Does the husband always ask his wife? It is important to recognize that this dependent behavior (whatever it is) is exhibited by the subject in the absence of restraining behavior by the stimulus.

8. *Competitive Behavior.* Again, we can only suggest an area of inquiry which seems to us to fall under this general rubric. Competitive behavior is indicated when the subject consistently attempts to better the efforts of the known stimulus. To what extent is the subject the rival of the known stimulus? BIs are collected about the responses of the subject to achieving and acquiring behavior by the known stimulus. Thus, the next door neighbor buys a bigger television set. What, if any, is the subject's response? What was the subject's response to his sibling when that sibling acquired something of value from his parent? What is the subject's behavior in competitive sports or games of any sort? How does he respond to defeat? The basic measure, "intensity," seems to us to be one of the most important for this variable.

9. *Physical Aggression.* This variable deals with the extent to which the subject physically attacks the known stimulus. BIs are collected about the subject's activities with the stim-

ulus in an attempt to discover if the subject physically assaults the known stimulus. This variable may not apply in many cases but we can see the need for it in other instances, e.g., siblings.

10. *Verbal Aggression.* Does the subject attack the stimulus with angry, caustic or sarcastic words? Does he manifest this behavior by the spoken and/or written word? Teasing behavior on the part of the subject toward the stimulus is also included, here. Does the subject talk against the stimulus to other persons? The innuendos of such behavior may be difficult to come by. Data under this variable can be accumulated by direct observation during the interview. Thus, the subject is asked to describe the known stimulus. Does he criticize the known stimulus? This line of inquiry then may lead to BIs of verbal aggression by the subject toward the known stimulus.

11. *Restraints.* This variable has to do with the extent to which the subject controls the behavior of the known stimulus. Does the subject's behavior interfere with the freedom of action of the stimulus? Is the subject's mere presence restricting to the stimulus? This variable should be distinguished from Dependent Behavior. In dependent behavior, the subject is responding with self-initiated behavior that may be on the opposite end of the continuum from restraining behavior. In one sense, dependent behavior can be considered yielding, and restraining behavior demanding. (It should be recognized that, in extremes, dependent behavior can also be considered restraining.) To obtain data for this variable, BIs are collected which have to do with the subject's efforts to control the behavior of the known stimulus.

12. *Sexual Behavior.* What is the sexual behavior of the subject toward the stimulus? Data are also obtained concerning sensuous and seductive behavior. This is a variable that is very often avoided by inexperienced Examiners. One must, for example, inquire concerning animal contacts of a sexual nature. BIs are collected about the physical behavior of the subject toward the known stimulus, e.g., the nature of the

embrace, movements of the subject such as dress-lifting or excessive touching.

13. Fear Behavior. This variable should be distinguished from avoidance behavior. Fear behavior is characterized by the following sorts of reactions to the stimulus: lack of counter-attack, either verbal or physical, to displays of aggression; and grossly observable physiologic reactions such as tremor, blushing and sweating. These are obviously more than simple avoidance of the known stimulus. Direct observation in the interview situation is a source of data for this variable. The subject, in describing the known stimulus, may by the nature of the description provide data about this variable. BIs need to be collected illustrative of Fear Behavior if it exists.

14. Deviant Behavior. This variable is obviously a catch-all. It is included to alert the Examiner to behaviors exhibited toward the known stimulus, by the subject, that vary markedly from expectancy. No description of this variable is included on the grounds that the Examiner is assumed to be skilled in detecting deviant behavior. However, it is necessary that supporting BIs be accumulated under this variable with respect to the behavior of a subject toward a particular known stimulus.

The reader will undoubtedly have noted that there is much overlap among the variables. At this stage of research the names we give the variables are relatively unimportant, but the data gathering is crucial if we are ever to cluster pieces of behavior in some meaningful fashion. The definition of variables has been brief for the simple reason that we do not know how to define them precisely. If BIs are collected and the basic measures applied to the kinds of behaviors indicated by the variables, the data will be obtained.

With respect to the stimulus categories, School, Work, Church, Subculture, Physical Environment and Unavoidable Illnesses and Accidents, data on the response side are obtained directly by collecting BIs. Thus, for School, the subject's responses to its Prestige, Social and Intellectual Demands and other stimulus variables will emerge from the BI technique. If BIs cannot be elicited, then the Examiner must resort to direct inquiry in order to obtain information about the subject's responses to the stimulus variables. These are S-R responses for coding purposes. Thus, S-R13.1-18 refers to the subject's responses to Prestige Demands (variable 18) of the known stimulus, First School (S13.1). The interview guide found in the appendix will facilitate this data gathering.

We have previously discussed stimulus categories, Scale A. Thereafter, we presented responses to these known stimuli, Scale B. We will now consider Scale C which consists of those responses to stimuli either not readily apparent or not identifiable in our present state of knowledge, called "Operant Responses" (OR). We have, on an *a priori* basis selected out 12 broad categories of operant responding as follows:

OR1.0	Oral Habits	OR7.0	Sexual Behavior
OR2.0	Sleeping	OR8.0	Social Behavior (general)
OR3.0	Elimination	OR9.0	Social Behavior (specific)
OR4.0	Cleanliness	OR10.0	Conforming Behavior
OR5.0	Motility	OR11.0	Level of Responding
OR6.0	Health	OR12.0	Other Nonoccupational Activities

For all of these categories there will be two or more subcategories. We will now attempt to define, briefly, each of these operant categories. As in our previous attempts, the definitions can only be suggestive. However, if the basic measures are attempted for each response class the data will be obtained.

OR1.0, ORAL HABITS

OR1.1 Eating. This class includes the ingestion of all substances, nutrient and non-nutrient. Data are obtained about the frequency, variety of foods, conditions of eating, in other words, all the basic measures are attempted. Additionally, data are obtained about the after-effects of eating, e.g., gas or heartburn, which define the basic measure "Correctness."

OR1.2 Drinking. The imbibing of all liquids is included in this class, water, milk, coffee, soft drinks, alcohol, etc. As with eating behavior, data are also obtained about the after-effects of drinking.

OR1.3 Smoking. Include cigarettes, pipe, chewing tobacco and tobacco substitutes. Collect data about after-effects.

OR2.0, SLEEPING

OR2.1 Sleeping. In addition to the basic measures, data are obtained about the positions assumed in sleeping. What is the frequency, duration, etc. of sleeping behavior, including naps. Although intensity as a measure may not be so obvious, we feel that it applies and can be estimated by amount of stimulation required to awaken the subject. Latency can be judged by time elapsing between going to bed and the onset of sleep. Inquiry concerning the conditions of sleep should reveal need of sleeping aids, clothing worn, ventilation, etc.

OR2.2 Dreaming. This class of responses is not amenable to direct observation except insofar as such behaviors as tossing, turning, nocturnal emission and crying out, may be related to dreaming. We are dependent, here, on the report of the subject. Inquiry is made concerning the frequency, intensity (vividness), variety and conditions of dreaming. Duration has to do with such data as "I dream all night" or "I dream after the alarm clock goes off." Content should, of course, be recorded.

OR3.0, ELIMINATION

OR3.1 Defecation. What is the frequency, latency, intensity and duration of defecating behavior? Inquiry is made concerning the conditions under which the subject defecates, e.g., only in his own home and need to read. The measure "Correctness" applies to the difficulty and other qualitative aspects of this response class.

OR3.2 Urination. Observations are made as above with "Defecation."

OR4.0, CLEANLINESS

OR4.1 Body Proper. This response class has to do with the cleanliness behavior directed toward the body other than hands, face, teeth and sex organs. Data are obtained about cleaning behavior, its frequency, intensity, duration, variety, conditions and efficiency. Information is collected about hair-washing behavior.

OR4.2 Hands and Face. These parts of the body are separated from the body proper because of the increased frequency of cleaning behavior directed toward them in our culture. The basic measures are applied. Data are collected about manicuring behavior.

OR4.3 Sex Organs. Direct inquiry is made about cleaning behavior directed toward the sex organs. The basic measures apply. In addition, data are obtained concerning cleaning behavior at the time of the menses and after sexual contact.

OR4.4 Teeth. The basic measures apply.

OR4.5 Clothes. Apply the basic measures to cleaning behavior directed toward clothes.

OR4.6 Living Quarters. Apply the basic measures to cleaning behavior directed toward the subject's room, house and work situation. BIs are obtained about whether or not the subject exhibits this behavior himself or gets others to do it for him.

OR4.7 Food and Drink. What is the subject's cleanliness behavior directed toward food and drink? What is the frequency, etc. with which he cleans his food and drink or requires others to do so? Data are obtained about the subject's cleanliness behavior directed toward utensils used in eating and drinking.

OR5.0, MOTILITY

OR5.1 Gross Bodily Movements. Gross bodily movements involve all of the body or large bodily segments, e.g., walking, running, twisting, turning, nodding, bending, throwing and dancing. These are distinguished from fine bodily movements such as finger tapping, facial twitching, tremor and nail-biting.

What is the frequency, rate, intensity, etc., with which the subject exhibits gross bodily movements? Gracefulness or awkwardness of movements are subsumed under the efficiency measure.

OR5.2 Fine Movements. Apply the basic measures to the behaviors suggested above for this response class.

OR5.3 Verbal Behavior. Apply the basic measures to this behavior. Bear in mind that appropriateness of verbal behavior is covered by such measures as efficiency and direction. The clinical concept of "affect" is covered by the basic measures, e.g., changes in intensity (loudness) get at presence or absence of affect if used with correctness.

OR6.0, HEALTH

OR6.1 Attention to Physical Well-Being. With what frequency does the subject visit a physician or dentist? How often does he use health aids? How much does he talk about his health? What is the intensity, the conditions and variety of ways he pays attention to his physical well-being? What is the correctness of these responses, e.g., is he hypochondriacal?

OR6.2 Illnesses and Accidents. Inquiry is made concerning the frequency and nature of illnesses and accidents. Data must be obtained in order for later judgement to be applied to determine whether or not these were avoidable. The attempt, here, is to get at such things as "accident proneness" or unusual susceptibility to illnesses. However, such a bias should not be prejudicial to data-gathering.

OR6.3 Menstruation. Data are obtained about the frequency, duration, intensity, etc. of the menstrual cycle. What are the ways in which the subject responds to the menses? Difficulties with the menstrual cycle should emerge if the basic measures are used. Does the subject use internal or external absorbents?

OR7.0, SEXUAL BEHAVIOR

OR7.1 Sexual-Seeking Behavior. Here, we are interested in those activities of the subject aimed at finding sexual objects, either heterosexual or otherwise. What is the frequency with which the subject attempts to find sexual objects? How much effort (intensity) does he put into this behavior? How much time (duration) does he spend at it? How many different sexual objects (variety) does the subject seek out? Under what conditions does he exhibit this behavior, e.g., always at a bar with drinks, at the beach or at a party? How efficient is he?

OR7.2 Heterosexual Behavior. Actual sexual contact is the object of study, here. Include fore-play or "heavy petting" which involves physical contact with the sexual apparatus. Inquiry is also made concerning the latency of erection of penis, clitoris or nipple, and the latency or presence or absence of orgasm.

OR7.3 Sexual Behavior — Other. Include, here, homosexual behavior, animal contacts and autoeroticism. Apply the basic measures. Also, obtain information about the latency of erection and presence or absence of orgasm as above.

OR8.0, SOCIAL BEHAVIOR (GENERAL)

OR8.1 Social Play. This rubric is essentially "party" behavior. Is the subject the life of the party or a wall-flower? Is the subject an initiator of parties, or is he a passive participant? With what frequency does the subject exhibit this type of behavior? What is the intensity of his responses? How about varieties of behaviors and parties attended? The basic measures should be attempted as with all responses classes.

OR8.2 Public Behavior. How often does the subject engage in public affairs such as a charity fund drive? Does he join civic organizations? What is the frequency, variety, intensity, etc. with which the subject responds? From this inquiry BIs should emerge which indicate whether or not the subject is a passive participant or an active initiator in such activities. Does he make public speeches? Is he a joiner?

OR8.3 Companionship-Seeking Activity (Nonsexual). At the operant level of responding, how much time does the subject spend in seeking companionship? If he is in a strange city by himself over a period of time, does he actively search for companions? One extreme of such behavior might be the "lone wolf" who may, nevertheless, be busily engaged in sexual-seeking behavior. What is the frequency, intensity, etc. of such behavior?

OR9.0, Social Behavior (Specific)

OR9.1 Behavior Toward Unknown People. On first contact, how does the subject react to various kinds of people? In a party, does he tend to gravitate towards younger people, older, peers? What sex does he approach? What is the frequency and intensity of such approach (or avoiding) behavior? What are the variety of his responses to various kinds of people? For instance, is there a differential response directed toward older male figures of authority as opposed to older females? In this rubric, we are attempting to get at operant level responding toward people of various kinds, younger and older people, same and opposite sex, peers, superiors and inferiors.

OR9.2 Behavior Toward Unknown Animals. As differentiated from responses to known animals, what is the subject's behavior toward a dog on the street, a horse in a riding stable, a rat in a laboratory or a mouse at home?

OR10.0, Conforming Behavior

OR10.1 Social. Does the subject's behavior generally follow that of the people about him? For instance, if he spends some time in England, does he quickly pick up the accent, adopt their dress and eating habits? These responses are to be differentiated from responses to the known subculture. Examples might make our meaning clearer. Thus, if the subject moves to a new community where golf is popular, does he very soon begin playing golf for the first time? If he moves to an area in which alcoholic liquors are illegal, does he then stop drinking alcohol, Does he quickly adopt changes in clothing styles, food fads, speech, e.g., beatnik? Inquiry should be directed toward the intensity, variety, frequency, etc. of such behaviors.

OR10.2 Intellectual. What is the subject's resistance to persuasion, suggestion and public appeal? Does he freely express his own opinions or does he "climb on the band wagon?" When he goes shopping is a salesman able to sell him things he doesn't need? Does he hold to the prevailing political opinions of those about him? If he is a scientist does he quickly begin researching in a new and popular area? Does he conform to the intellectual behavior of people about him?

OR11.0, LEVEL OF RESPONDING

OR11.1 Alertness to Cue Change. There is a broad spectrum of stimuli to which a person may respond. The width of this spectrum varies with the individual. Some persons respond to a wide variety of stimulus changes. Others only respond to a narrow band of stimuli. For instance, there is a mathematician who seems to respond only to a blackboard and a piece of chalk, seemingly unresponsive to other stimuli. On the other end of such a continuum might be the "paranoid" person who is responsive to minute changes in the environment. The basic measures that seem important, here, are frequency, latency, variety, conditions, intensity and correctness. Take the case of a subject crossing a busy street. He may blunder across without any concern for oncoming vehicles. He may be overly hesitant and then dart across dangerously. What are the conditions under which the subject will be responsive?

OR11.2 Response to Stress. How does the subject respond to stresses such as examinations, near-miss automobile accidents, threat to well-being, either physical or psychological? Inquiry is made concerning emergencies encountered by the subject and his reactions to them. The basic measures seem to be intensity, latency, variety (of responses), conditions (nature of the emergency) and, most importantly, correctness.

OR11.3 Work Level. What is the subject's operant level of working? For instance, does the student study rapidly or slowly (rate)? Does he need certain environmental conditions to apply before he can study? Does he study efficiently in terms of the results of his study? How easily can he be distracted (intensity)? How many different ways does he study (variety)? Apply this same line of inquiry to all working behavior.

OR12.0, OTHER NONOCCUPATIONAL ACTIVITIES

OR12.1 Hobbies and Avocations. This rubric includes secondary jobs and serious hobbies. Inquiry is made concerning whether or not the subject has a source of income other than the primary source. Does he have any hobbies? These could range from raising orchids to stamp-collecting to weight-lifting. Apply the basic measures to such activities.

OR12.2 Solitary Behavior. This response class is an attempt to get at the subject's behavior when he is alone, activities other than those previously defined. Thus, does the subject admire himself in the mirror when naked or otherwise? How much time does he spend grooming himself? Does he have a tendency to shut himself off from people for any particular activity? Is he a lone drinker? Is he an omnivorous reader? Detailed inquiry is made concerning the nature of the subject's behavior when he is completely alone.

OR12.3 Hoarding Behavior. Is the subject a collector? To what extent does the subject collect such objects as cars, boats, magazines, money, clothes and bottle tops? Does the subject "never throw anything away?"

OR12.4 Driving Behavior. What is the subject's behavior in driving cars, boats, planes, motorbikes, bicycles, horses and other means of transportation?

We cannot emphasize too strongly the importance of applying the basic measures to each of the operant response classes. It is obvious that not all of the basic measures are applicable to each class. Thus, the basic measure *rate* does not seem to us to apply to sleeping behavior, but most of the other measures do. If the Examiner becomes accustomed to thinking in terms of the basic measures he will necessarily obtain the required data in terms of BIs.

The method of investigation we are proposing is one that is hedged in by a number of problems. It requires a careful, painstaking approach — more of the scientific method, we feel, than other, more circumscribed procedures. In laboratory studies, dependent and independent variables can usually be more precisely defined and replication is, therefore, relatively easy. Investigation of gross human behavior, as we are proposing it, makes for difficulty in replication unless strict adherence to sound methodological principles is followed.

There are two broad classes of problems that occur to us. The first of these is concerned with the obtaining of valid data. The second class of problems emerges when an attempt is made to *apply* the Scales. This chapter will concern itself with a discussion of these problems.

We are very conscious of the fact that data obtained from the interview are usually suspect. Therefore, an important methodological problem is that of obtaining valid data. As we have indicated in a previous chapter, consistency of verbal report in describing BIs is of prime importance in establishing the validity of the data. Crucial, here, is the experience of the Examiner. It has been our finding that with enough patience and skill, the data, insofar as they are remembered by the subject, will emerge. Nevertheless, there remains the problem of the fallibility of memory. This problem requires that, whenever possible, corroborating data be obtained from persons who know or have known the subject sufficiently to describe BIs about him and the stimulus categories of interest. In connection with this point it is obvious that the younger the subject within limits the more likely it is that corroborating data can be obtained. It follows from the above discussion that, whenever possible, it is well to obtain subjects who are known to others so that valid information can be accumulated.

There remains, nevertheless, the problem of the subject about whom only scanty or no corroborating information can be obtained. The question arises as to whether or not valid data can be secured under these circumstances. Our answer to this question is that valid data can be obtained providing certain conditions are met. The same criteria are applied to these data as to any other data in psychology. First, we ask, are the data internally consistent? BIs reported by the informant must not be contradictory. Next, are the data plausible? To be plausible the data must be acceptable within the limits of what is now known about human behavior. If the subject reports that he was reared on the planet Mars for the first ten years of his life, this report, although, it is not plausible, is of interest, especially if such statements are made consistently. In such a case, internal consistency is satisfied but plausibility is not, and no valid data are obtained about the first ten years of life. Thirdly, are the obtained data lawful? In other words, do the data follow known principles of human behavior? For instance, does the subject report BIs about father that are extremely negative, but also report BIs between him and father that are positive. Thus, in reporting BIs about father he cites incidents showing his father drunk, quarrelsome and avoidant of the family. However, in reporting incidents between himself and father, father is described as exhibiting many displays of affection and many activities with the subject.

The fourth and most important criterion of validity is, it seems to us, the relationship between reported data and observable behavior of public knowledge on the part of the subject and individuals of like status. This criterion overlaps, of course, with plausibility and lawfulness. It is, in any psychological investigation, the ultimate, overriding criterion. For instance, are the found data (obtained by the interview method) consistently related to incarceration for public drunkenness, to commitment to a mental hospital or to the presence of ulcer? The question, here, is whether or not the subject's report of his behavior agrees with an objectively observable criterion. If it does, then the data are valid and, by definition, reliable.

In summary, then the criteria to be applied to the data obtained by the interview method are as follows:

1. Internal consistency
2. Plausibility
3. Lawfulness
4. Agreement with an objective criterion.

In the sort of investigations suggested by us, the question often arises as to whether or not the same data could not be obtained by simpler and less time-consuming methods. It might seem as if the information demanded by the P-J Scales could be just as easily, or more easily secured on a larger number of cases by the questionnaire method. In order to test this possibility a questionnaire was constructed using sensitive items from the P-J Scales. (An abbreviated form of the questionnaire and the results obtained by using it will be found in Table 1.) This questionnaire, tested for reading comprehen-

TABLE 1—*Questionnaire Results Contrasting the Answers of Workhouse Alcoholics (N=30) and College Students (N=45)*

	Per Cent Answering "Yes"	
Father	Alcoholics	Students
1. Did you see your father much during the first ten years of your life?	83	84
2. Did your father beat you more than he should have during your first ten years?	7	18
3. Was your father kind to you?	100	92
4. Did your father work steadily?	100	91
5. Did your father take good care of you?	100	87
6. Was your father's health good?	86	82
7. Did your father go to church regularly?	67	62
8. Did your father have many friends?	93	82
9. Did your father drink much liquor?	17	20
10. Was your father ever in a mental hospital?	7	2
11. Did your father ever get in trouble with the law?	3	7
12. Did your father ever beat your mother?	10	8
13. Did your father and mother have many arguments?	11	42

TABLE 1—*Continued*

Mother	Per Cent Answering "Yes"	
	Alcoholics	Students
1. Did you see your mother much during the first ten years of your life?	93	93
2. Did your mother beat you more than she should have?	7	4
3. Was your mother kind to you?	97	95
4. Did your mother work steadily?	12	33
5. Did your mother take good care of you?	100	95
6. Was your mother's health good?	93	93
7. Did your mother go to church regularly?	90	73
8. Did your mother have many friends?	87	93
9. Did your mother drink much liquor?	0	0
10. Was your mother ever in a mental hospital?	7	0
11. Did your mother ever get in trouble with the law?	0	2
Sibs		
1. Did you have any brothers or sisters in the first ten years of your life?	93	87
2. Did you play much with any of your brothers and sisters?	92	64
Peers		
1. Did you have many friends during the first ten years of your life?	100	91
2. Did you play games and do things together regularly?	100	91
Other Relatives		
1. Did you see much of your other relatives in the first ten years of your life?	78	80
2. Were they kind to you?	100	93

sion on a population similar to workhouse alcoholics, was administered to 45 college students and 30 workhouse alcoholics. The results obtained showed, very strikingly, that the workhouse alcoholics report *less* "deprived" backgrounds than the college students. Of 30 items, the alcoholics reported less deprivation on 20, tied the college students on three and reported more deprivation on seven. Using the binomial expansion, counting hits when the alcoholics reported less deprivation (splitting the ties evenly), the probability obtained is .02. This finding is contrary to fact and theory as we now know it.

Thus, in answer to the question, "Did your father take good care of you?" 100 per cent of the alcoholics responded that he did, whereas only 87 per cent of the college students answered "yes." Our studies, to be summarized in the next chapter, indicate that the workhouse alcoholics had fathers who were punitive, avoidant and unprotective of their offspring. In answer to the question, "Did your father and mother have many arguments?" 11 per cent of the alcoholics responded "yes," whereas 42 per cent of the students responded affirmatively. Again, these results are in contradiction with our findings based on intensive interview with the P-J Scales. These results clearly violate our criteria of plausibility and agreement with an objective criterion. It seems to us that the questionnaire method does *not* lend itself to the kinds of investigations we are suggesting, except insofar as obtaining data about such factual items as hours of sleep, frequency of eating and the like. However, we suggest the questionnaire approach be used with caution even for such items. We have found that a seemingly straightforward item such as frequency of contact with a parent is often overestimated on a questionnaire.

Another plaguing problem is delimiting cross-sectional behavior. Generally, what we mean by the phrase "cross-sectional behavior" is a sample of behaviors at a particular time in the life of the subject. It is fairly common to study "current" cross-sectional behavior, i.e., the subject's responses to stimulus situations at the time of observation. Thus, observations of children at play, for instance, will often be accomplished by observations over specified times, e.g., five minutes. Barker and Wright's study (1954) of the responses of a child over a single day is another example of a cross-sectional study. Our problem, however, is different. Much of the behavior in which we are interested cannot be directly observed. Also, the time sample must be much greater in order for the behaviors with which we are concerned to emerge. In a current cross-sectional study with the P-J Scales, the time covered by the study in the interview setting will vary depending on the stimulus or response class. If, for instance, a subject has not seen his grandmother for six months, then we are interested in his and her behavior at the last contact. If he sees her regularly every six months then we also are interested in the last several contacts in order to establish any consistency of behavior. The assumption, here, is that the grandmother (when living) constitutes a current stimulus for the subject even if he sees her only every six months. By the same token, his reactions to her are part of his current response patterns. Similarly, if we are inquiring concerning operant responses, we need to go back in time in order to establish the consistency of current behavior. For example, with sleeping behavior we do not simply inquire about the previous night but, rather, obtain enough BIs to describe accurately the subject's sleeping behavior.

We must admit that we cannot, at the present writing, define cross-sectional behavior in an entirely satisfactory manner. Thus, we are observing a college freshman. Six months ago he was a high school student. For some behaviors we are not interested in what he did prior to coming to college, for others we might be. In high school, he was a football player. In college, he is not out for football. Many of his behaviors have changed as a result of this change in environment and status. On the other hand, in studying his heterosexual behavior, we might have to go back in time more than six months in order to establish consistency. Generally speaking, major changes in status and/or environment will serve as guides in delimiting cross-sectional observations. The crucial point in obtaining cross-sectional data is to collect sufficient data so that given the current stimulus situation the response can be predicted with a high degree of probability.

The usual longitudinal approach is a running account of a subject's experiences during the course of life. Our approach differs in that the P-J Scales are applied to a particular *segment* of life. In studying the first few years of life, we have taken the age of ten at which to apply the Scales. However, in so doing we have had to obtain data from the years preceding this age in order to obtain consistency and completeness. So far, in our research, we have been, for the most part, limited to interview of the subject, himself, and, therefore, restricted by the subject's ability to recall. Our experience has been that only rare subjects remember much about their life prior to age five. Our cross-sectional studies of the first ten years of life, which will be reported in the next chapter, are really cross-sectional studies at the age of ten, but with sufficient data from the previous years of the subject's life so that in effect the data are based on all that the subject can remember of the first ten years of his life. If further data are to be obtained about a subject, then a cross-sectional study is made of him at the age of, for instance, 15 with suficient data from previous years to establish consistency at that age. The point we wish to make is that, with the P-J Scales, cross-sectional studies can be made for any segment of life. They need to be cross-sectional, in our sense of the term, in order to obtain the data demanded by the Scales.

The usual longitudinal study does not insist on the identification of specific stimuli and the responses to them. For our approach, a longitudinal study would consist of a series of cross-sectional studies taken at different points in the life history of the subject. What these points in the life history are, we do not know. We feel sure, however, that crucial environmental changes will guide the choice of life segments to be studied. Much, of course, will depend on the age of the subject and the availability of informants with knowledge of the subject's behavior. In any case, enough data must be obtained in order to establish behavioral patterns, thus, again bringing us back to our point concerning the flexibility of what constitutes cross-sectional behavior.

In any attempt to apply the Scales experimentally, a number of special problems arise. The first of these is concerned with establishing useful base-lines of behavior for the purpose of comparing behaviors from person to person or group to group.

This problem becomes obvious when we attempt to determine if the behavior of a particular individual differs significantly from the behavior of his peers of like status. For instance, do Displays of Affection exhibited by an eight-year-old boy toward father occur with significantly less frequency than similar behavior displayed by his peers of like status? We do not, at present, have the data to make such comparisons. Further discussion of this problem as it concerns deviant behavior can be found elsewhere (Pascal, 1959).

Another methodological problem is concerned with the choice of subjects. Target populations are, of course, determined by the problem under investigation. If a target population is to be exhaustively studied, cross-sectionally, no particular problems are encountered. For example, it is decided to contrast the cross-sectional behavior of patients of two wards in a given mental hospital. The problem becomes complicated when we attempt to study less well defined populations, e.g., "normal" subjects. In view of the fact that we do not know what constitutes normalcy of behavior, our approach has been to contrast individuals characterized by less deviant behavior with those exhibiting grossly deviant behavior. In the absence of knowledge of base-line behavior, we have crudely separated populations based on some objective and commonly accepted criteria such as being inmates of the county workhouse for repeated public drunkeness as opposed to subjects lacking this characteristic, similarly with psychotic patients in a mental hospital. Obvious limitations are applied to control ("normal") subjects such as recent discharge from a mental hospital, extremely asocial behavior and brain damage. It has been our practice to match the less deviant (controls) with the more deviant (experimental subjects) on such variables as sex, age, education, socio-economic status and intellectual status.

In any study in which it is desired to contrast two groups, the attempt is made to spread the two groups apart as far as possible on the dependent variable at least in the early stages of research. Thus, in studying duodenal ulcer patients, these are matched on the variables previously mentioned with nonulcer cases. This procedure only *seems* to spread the two groups apart. The two extremes of the continuum "ulcer-nonulcer" can be contaminated by a great number of variables. For example, the nonulcer control may exhibit some other form of behavioral deviancy such as alcoholism. This is an obvious point. What concerns us, however, are the more subtle contaminating variables. For instance, in a recent study by one of our students, Lothrop (1958), five duodenal ulcer patients were matched with five patients without duodenal ulcer. In order to obtain five patients who were relatively free of "psychosomatic" disorders, it was necessary for the physician to screen over 100 cases. Even after such screening one or two of these five controls were suspect as far as psychogenic factors were concerned. Such a beginning approach in research does not preclude the later contrasting of groups more alike on the dependent variable. It is our contention that in the early stages of systematic observation the independent variables will emerge much more clearly if the experimental and control groups are spread as far apart as possible on the dependent variable.

In research using the P-J Scales the investigator is confronted with the need to decide the stage of life to be studied, the stimulus categories, responses and variables to employ. The problem under investigation and the subjects to be used will, for the most part, determine what parts of the P-J Scales to use. Not all the stimulus categories, responses and variables of the Scales need to be applied to all subjects. A selection may be made. For instance, it is desired to study whether or not generalization of response to father in the first ten years of life occurs in later life to older males or figures of authority. In such a study, the stimulus category of major interest would be father and his characteristics (stimulus variables) in the first ten years of the subject's life. The study would also focus on the subject's responses to father during the first ten years of life. Ideally, the dependent variable in such a study would involve the systematic observation of the subject's responses (as an adult) to older males under experimental conditions. (Another method would be to study the subject's cross-sectional behavior, by interview of the subject and older males with whom he is in frequent contact.) Obviously, the study would need to vary the behaviors of the experimental stimuli along a continuum of similarity to father's behavior during the first ten years of the subject's life.

The Scales can also be used in validating studies as the criterion. Thus, it is desired to determine how behavior in a miniature life situation in the laboratory is related to behavior outside the laboratory. A child of six is exposed to his peers in a laboratory play situation and his behavior systematically observed. To what extent is such behavior related to his reactions to his siblings or peers in the home situation and everyday contact? The part of the P-J Scales to be used in such a study would be the stimulus categories siblings and peers, the responses to them and operant behavior toward peers, obtained by interview of parents and others who know the subject well.

In some of our preliminary studies we have discovered that stimulus variables, for certain stimulus categories, that have to do with actual physical contact with the subject for the first ten years of his life, are significantly related to adult behavior. Such stimulus variables as Play Activities, Restraints, Physical Punishment and Displays of Affection on the part of. the stimulus categories, Parents and Siblings, have yielded significant relationships with later behavior in a number of studies. In view of such findings it may be desired to study only these stimulus variables across a large number of stimulus categories and for a larger population than would be possible with more intensive study. A comparison can be made between the effects of these variables as opposed to the effects of a different cluster of stimulus variables. The study could be concerned with the subject's reactions to affection as an adult as a function of affection displayed toward him as a child.

The point we are making is that the entire P-J Scales do

not have to be used in any particular investigation. They can be used by individual stimulus categories, individual stimulus variables, separate response variables to particular known stimulus categories, segments of operant behavior and various combinations of these. The extent to which reliable and valid data can be obtained, the nature of the subject population and the problem determine the parts of the P-J Scales to use and the parts to be left out.

REFERENCES

Barker, R. G., and Wright, H. F.: Midwest and its Children. White Plains, New York, Row, Peterson and Co., 1954.

Lothrop, W. W.: The Relationship Between Experimental Variables and the Occurence of Duodenal Ulcer. Unpublished Ph.D. dissertation, University of Tennessee, 1958.

Pascal, G. R.: Behavioral Change in the Clinic: A Systematic Approach. New York, Grune & Stratton, 1959.

Methodological Investigations

Approximately 100 subjects have been interviewed using the P-J Scales in substantially their present form. We feel it important to give the reader the benefit of our experiences by reporting some of the early work using this approach. In this chapter, therefore, we will report actual experimentation using the Scales and, in the process, consider such problems as reliability and quantification of the data.

Scoring. In the absence of base-line data, a method had to be devised to order the data numerically. Our solution to this problem was to devise a simple rating scale. Each variable is scaled on a three point basis. The rating of "3" is reserved for behavior appropriate to an individual's status in a particular subculture. Obviously, to give such a rating, E must have knowledge of the range of occurrence of behaviors in the particular subculture. Thus, the range of behaviors for the subculture, Greenwich Village, New York City, may be different from the range for the subculture, East Tennessee Mountain Country. The rating is based on a knowledge of expectancy for a given subculture and also on a knowledge of expectancy for an individual of given status in that subculture, e.g., expectancy would be different for a minister and an unskilled worker. In the absence of data on such matters, the rating is clearly judgmental. A rating of "1" is always given if the deviation from cultural or status expectancy is great, regardless of direction. Thus, an individual would receive a rating of "1" for an exaggerated display of affection just as he would for no display of affection. In other words, "1" is used for extremes of behavior, either too little or too much. If E bears in mind that the rating "1" is given for extremes of behavior, he will have little difficulty in using this end of the scale. Some behaviors will fall between the ratings of "3" and "1." For such cases the rating of "2" is used.

There are a large number of variables that are directly quantifiable. For instance, such variables as number of hours of sleep, frequency of intercourse, elimination, contact with parents, etc., are stated in actual numbers. Although these variables will also be rated on a three-point scale, the numbers should be recorded as a basis for the ratings. Eventually, it is on the basis of actual data that base-lines will be determined for various subcultures and individuals of given status within the subculture.

In addition to the ratings "1, 2, 3," three other scoring categories were used. When the stimulus was absent, such as a grandparent being dead prior to the subject's birth, the rating "0" was employed. If the data about a variable were nonexistent or meager so that a rating could not be given with confidence, the variable was scored "No Data" (ND). One other scoring category was found necessary to order the data. Some variables were not applicable to the subject under study, for instance, restraints put upon a much older sibling by a much younger one. Under these circumstances, the variable was designated "Does Not Apply" (DA). Thus, for each variable, the following scoring categories were used:

0—stimulus absent.
1—marked deviation of behavior from expectancy.
2—behavior falling between the ratings "1" and "3."
3—behavior according to expectancy.
ND—no data.
DA—variable does not apply.

We have found a tendency in our students to concentrate on the rating rather than fully reporting the data obtained. It cannot be emphasized too strongly that the technique of data gathering that is basic to our approach, the behavioral incident, should be fully reported, not the opinion or attitudes of the subject *or* the Examiner. Unless the data are fully reported, no reliability studies can be accomplished.

Reliability. For the type of research we are reporting, the problem of reliability is crucial. The problem revolves around the need for E to obtain sufficient data for each variable so that an independent observer can confidently rate the data. Obviously, the crux of the matter is for E to leave his own bias out of the data. The report of the interview *must be factual.* If it is not, then any reliability study will be spurious. Words implying value judgments, clinical impressions and dynamic interpretations are not factual and must be deleted from any report of interview submitted for study when the data are to be rated.

There is another problem of bias which, although it may well be considered a validity matter, is pertinent to the immediate discussion. This is, essentially, the well-known problem of "halo" which plagues any ratings. Thus, when E begins to rate a subject, he is apt to begin with the Grandparents and continue on to Mother, Father, Siblings, etc. The ratings given early in the process may well influence those given later, e.g., if Mother is down-graded, then the ratings given may influence judgments of Father and Siblings. In order to counteract this effect, it is suggested that ratings be given across subjects by stimulus categories. For instance, rate all fathers across all subjects, then Mother, etc. It is assumed, here, that all identifying information about important dependent variables is deleted, e.g., whether or not a subject is an alcoholic. In this connection, another possible contaminating process is one in which ratings are made on the first ten years of life *and* on cross-sectional behavior, on the same subject. Thus, a subject down-graded on the ratings of the first ten years of life is apt to be down-graded on ratings of cross-sectional behavior unless precautions are taken so that the "halo" effect is minimized.

The studies we are reporting differ from the usual approaches in the treatment of reliability. Most reliability studies deal with a large number of subjects and fewer variables. However, in our studies, we are typically faced with a large number of variables and a small number of subjects. Our problem is to determine whether or not judges agree on the deviancy or expectancy of the reported BIs as a basis for rating the variable. Therefore, in estimating reliability, we have been primarily concerned with the agreement between judges on the individual variables. From such a procedure there naturally emerges an estimate of the agreement across subjects.

Davis (1959) computed reliability on the P-J Scales by testing the agreement for two judges of the reported data by variables for each stimulus category. Rank correlations were computed by variables for each of the stimulus categories, Grandparents, Mother, Father, Siblings and Peers. For five workhouse alcoholics and their five matched controls a total of 50 correlation coefficients were computed. The rhos obtained ranged from .76 to .98 with a median of .88.

In a reliability study cited in the Annual Report of the Alcoholism Research Project of the University of Tennessee Psychological Service Center (1959), agreement between judges was estimated by computing per cent agreement of ratings of all stimulus variables for each subject. Each subject was rated by two judges. There were 80 variables for each subject. Table 2 shows the extent of agreement between judges. It can

TABLE 2—*Per Cent Agreement Between Independent Judges in Rating Variables of the P-J Scales for County Workhouse Alcoholics*

Subject	Per Cent Complete Agreement	Per Cent Differing by One Point	Per Cent Differing by Two Points
1	84	13	3
2	70	24	6
3	81	14	5
4	76	21	3
Total	78	18	4

be seen that there was perfect agreement in 78 per cent of the ratings. There was a difference of one point in 18 per cent of the ratings. This displacement occurred primarily between the ratings "2" and "3." There were reversals between "1" and "3" in only four per cent of the ratings. Inspection of the data revealed that there was practically no disagreement on the categories "0," "ND" and "DA."

Mullen (1959) rated 49 stimulus variables of the P-J Scales for each of nine duodenal ulcer cases. His agreement with an independent judge is shown in Table 3. The results agree with those of the previous, similar study with alcoholics.

TABLE 3—*Per Cent Agreement Between Independent Judges in Rating Variables of the P-J Scales for Duodenal Ulcer Cases (Mullen, 1959)*

Subject	Per Cent Complete Agreement	Per Cent Differing by One Point	Per Cent Differing by Two Points
1	80	20	0
2	85	15	0
3	75	25	0
4	70	30	0
5	80	19	1
6	84	16	0
7	65	35	0
8	78	20	2
9	87	13	0
Mean	78.2	21.4	.3

In spite of the fact that there are no base-line data on which to base expectancy, the three studies cited show that high reliability can be obtained by using the P-J Scales in the manner suggested. We feel that the high reliability obtained is due to intimate knowledge of the subculture of the subjects by the raters. All raters had extensive experience in intensive interviewing of the members of the subculture. Additional factors which contributed to high reliability are:

1. The "0" category, which indicates absence of the stimulus, is perfectly reliable.

2. The differentiation between the rating of "1" and "3" is usually quite clear in the data, since the rating "1" is only given for *marked* deviation from expectancy (the reliability of the "1" rating is almost perfect).

3. Little disagreement was found between judges for the ratings "ND" and "DA."

Quantitative Considerations. The ratings obtained from the P-J Scales present a number of problems in quantitative analysis. Some of these will have to remain unsolved in our present state of knowledge. The method of analysis we will present is based on the belief that the grossness of the data does not warrant refined statistical treatment. We feel that the statistical treatment employed reflects the differences inherent in the data.

Once the ratings have been ascertained for all variables under study, a table is prepared listing the ratings of the variables by the individual subject and by the stimulus category. If, then, it is desired to study a single variable such as Displays of Affection by Father in the first ten years of the subject's life, a table is prepared listing the ratings of this variable across individual pairs of matched subjects as follows:

Ratings of Displays of Affection (Father)

Subject Pair	Controls	Exp.
1	2	1
2	2	1
3	0	1
4	3	0
5	2	ND
6	3	1
7	3	0
8	ND	1
9	ND	1
10	3	1

The table is inspected to determine the frequency of the ND category. Obviously, if this category is too frequent the variable cannot discriminate between experimental and control subjects. When, for a given subject, a high frequency of the ND category is encountered across all variables and all stimulus categories, the data for this subject cannot be used and the subject has to be discarded. This result can be due to either an inexperienced E or an uncooperative subject. We have had few such experiences. It is possible that such a result can be obtained from an extremely compulsive judge who might demand BIs ad infinitum before making a rating.

It will be noted that the table contains three "0" entries. It will be recalled that "0" indicates absence of the stimulus, in this case, Father. Is absence of the father in the first ten years of life "better" or "worse" than the presence of a father deviant

("1") on the variable? In counting the number of times deviancy was exhibited on the variable, the rating "0" was counted on the side of more deviancy. The final answer to this question awaits further research.

Inspection of the table shows that the rating of "1" occurs only, and is the modal value, in the experimental subjects, whereas "2" and "3" predominate in the column of control subjects with "3" being the modal value. In order to determine whether or not a significant difference exists between the experimental and control subjects, the binomial expansion was applied. There are three pairs in which the ND category occurs, which leaves seven pairs for statistical treatment. Of these seven pairs, the numerical value for the control subjects is higher in six of them. Making the assumption that there is a fifty-fifty chance for one rating to exceed the other for each pair, the binomial expansion yields a probability of .062 for six out of seven events being in the same direction. (We have, in practice, not used those pairs in which the ND category appears. This may be a questionable procedure since it may be that the ND category and the "0" rating will turn out to be equivalent.)

The example above shows the method of analysis used when experimental and control groups are contrasted for a given variable. Such an analysis is done for every variable. Further analysis, then, depends on the objectives of the investigation. If the purpose of the research is to study the characteristics of stimulus categories, as in the research we will report, then the analysis proceeds to the combining of variables by stimulus categories. Thus, if we are interested in contrasting the Fathers of the control subjects with those of the experimental subjects in order to determine which received the more deviant ratings, we would average the ratings for all variables for Father, excluding the ND rating. We would then have a single numerical value for the Father of each subject. Considering the data by pairs, the question then becomes how many Fathers of controls have higher average ratings than the Fathers of experimental subjects, and the binomial would be applied as in the example given. This analysis, if it shows a significant difference, allows us to examine the individual variables with more confidence.

We might then be interested in determining the significance of a single variable across all stimulus categories. Take any variable of interest such as the Religious Behavior of Grandparents and Parents. For each subject, total the ratings for the variable across these stimulus categories and average, again excluding the ND rating. As a result of this procedure there should be a single numerical value for each subject. Thereafter, experimental and control subjects can be contrasted, applying the binomial as above. Appendix 2 presents an actual example showing how ratings are combined across stimulus categories and across variables.

The reader is reminded that the procedure outlined above (and used in our illustrative data in Appendix 2) is expedient and offered as a stop-gap until such time as enough data are available to establish base-lines of behavior. Therefore, the primary emphasis should be on data-gathering, not on the ratings. We see at least two steps to be accomplished before we can really quantify the data: (1) the accumulation of a large number of specific, operationally defined pieces of behavior, and (2) the ordering of these data into meaningful clusters and quantitative values. Some of the data we now collect are directly quantifiable and directly amenable to the establishment of expectancies, e.g., number of hours of sleep, frequency of eating, frequency of contact with a particular stimulus category, etc. Other behaviors of interest such as Providing Behavior are not, at present, quantifiable. Specific behaviors need to be accumulated and clusters established which will later be named. At the present stage of research, we do not feel that refined statistical treatment of the data is warranted. Computations of intercorrelations of the variables and studies of their interaction are, as yet, premature. Not until we get the data will such studies be appropriate.

The method of data treatment presented, crude as it is, allows for experimental studies at the same time that data are being gathered. Our next section will demonstrate this point.

A Study of Workhouse Alcoholics. Nine male county workhouse alcoholics who had a history of at least five arrests for public drunkeness were individually matched for sex, age, education, intellectual capacity and vocation with nine controls who had a history of little or no alcoholic consumption. Each subject was intensively interviewed using the P-J Scales. An attempt was made to obtain BIs concerning the characteristics of important persons encountered by the subjects during the first ten years of their lives. These important people (stimulus categories) on whom sufficient data were obtainable turned out to be grandparents, parents, siblings and peers. From the data obtained by interview an attempt was made to rate each stimulus variable of the P-J Scales (Davis, 1959). (The reliability of these ratings is reported in a previous section.) The ratings for the stimulus categories of experimental and control subjects were contrasted by pairs, as illustrated in Appendix II.

A second experiment was conducted in which 10 additional county workhouse alcoholics were contrasted with 10 additional controls. The same procedure for matching, rating and contrasting pairs was employed as in the first experiment. Tables 4 and 5 show the results obtained for each experiment when the ratings are combined and averaged by stimulus category. (See the section on Quantitative Considerations.) Table

TABLE 4—*Results of Experiment I with Alcoholics. Summary of Mean Stimulus Ratings—First 10 Years of Life*
(3 is average expectancy, 2 intermediate and 1 deviant)

	Experimental	Control	P value
Grandparents	1.6	2.4	.02
Mother	1.6	2.7	.002
Father	1.1	2.8	.002
Siblings	1.4	2.4	.02
Peers	1.7	2.7	.002
Totals	1.5	2.6	.00003

TABLE 5—*Results of Experiment II with Alcoholics. Summary of Mean Stimulus Ratings—First 10 Years of Life*
(3 is average expectancy, 2 intermediate and 1 deviant)

	Experimental	Control	P value
Grandparents	0.7	1.1	.05
Mother	1.4	2.9	.001
Father	1.1	2.6	.01
Siblings	1.2	2.7	.01
Peers	.8	3.0	.11
Totals	1.0	2.5	.0003

6 shows the individual stimulus variables that remain significant (.01 level) across both experiments. It should be noted that although the controls had higher ratings than the experimentals for all stimulus categories by a factor of two, the grandparents and peers were discarded from Table 6 because they did not meet the required level of significance across both experiments.

TABLE 6—*Mean Ratings of Stimulus Variables Significant in Both Alcoholism Experiments*

	Mother		Father		Sibs		Means	
	E	C	E	C	E	C	E	C
1. Frequency of contact	1.8	2.8	—	—	—	—	—	—
2. Activities	.9	2.7	.8	2.7	1.1	2.7	.9	2.7
3. Displays of affection	1.1	2.6	.7	2.6	—	—	.9	2.6
4. Providing behavior	1.4	3.0	—	—	—	—	—	—
5. Restraints	1.0	2.8	.9	2.6	—	—	1.0	2.7
6. Physical punishment	—	—	1.0	2.7	—	—	—	—
11. Religious behavior	1.3	2.6	.7	2.6	—	—	1.0	2.6
13. Compatible behavior	1.5	2.9	.8	2.9	1.0	2.3	1.1	2.7
17. Deviant behavior	—	—	1.0	2.9	—	—	—	—

Although primarily methodological, these findings suggest that the ratings for the experimental subjects' Mothers, Fathers and Siblings deviate from expectancy more than those of the control subjects. An interpretation of the data based on the definitions of the significantly differentiating stimulus variables suggests that the experimental subjects were more "deprived" psychologically than the control subjects during the first ten years of life. The specifics of this "psychological deprivation" can be clearly seen in Table 6. The details of these experiments are published elsewhere (Pascal and Jenkins, 1960).

A Comparison of Alcoholics, Psychotics, Duodenal Ulcer Cases and Controls. Ten psychotics (inmates of a mental hospital and carrying the psychiatric diagnosis of schizophrenia) and nine duodenal ulcer cases from Mullen's study *(ibid)* were matched on the variables previously mentioned with both the control and experimental subjects of the second alcoholism study. For the stimulus categories Mother, Father and Siblings a study similar to the alcoholism investigation was accomplished contrasting the controls with the psychotics. A further study contrasted the controls with the duodenal ulcer patients (Mullen, *ibid*). Finally, all possible cross comparisons were made between the four groups, controls, alcoholics, psychotics and duodenal ulcer cases. Additionally, all subjects were administered the University of Tennessee Deprivation Scale, which is a crude estimate of the subject's current functioning in his environment, a high score indicating considerable stimulus deprivation.*

Table 7 shows the results obtained. The detailed data showing subject pairs by stimulus variables and stimulus categories can be found elsewhere (Annual Report of Alcoholism Research, 1959, Pascal and Jenkins, *ibid;* Mullen, *ibid*). The over-all mean ratings shown at the bottom of Table 7 indicate gross disparity between the means for alcoholics and controls, whereas the psychotic and ulcer patients tend to be similar and less divergent from the controls. This trend holds for Mother, Father and Siblings.

*There are 16 variables on the scale, each scored either "0" or "1," "1" indicating current environmental deprivation and "0" indicating absence of environmental deprivation. The score on the Deprivation Scale consists of a summation of the number of "ones." Maximum score on the Scale is 16, indicating relatively complete environmental deprivation. The items of the Scale follow: Employment, Income, Debts, Fear, Wife, Parents, Children, Other Relatives, Church, Other Organizations, Friends, Job Participation, Job Status, Status-Other, Residence and Education. The data are obtained from individual interview.

This Scale was first developed in connection with research on duodenal ulcer at the Veterans Administration Hospital, Atlanta, Georgia. The research was later sponsored by the Department of Surgery, the Veterans Administration. Members of the research team are J. C. Thoroughman, M.D., Project Director, James Crutcher, M.D., and the authors.

TABLE 7—*Mean Ratings Across All Stimulus Variable for the First 10 Years of Life: Contrasting Alcoholics, Psychotics, Duodenal Ulcer Patients and Controls*

(Range in parentheses)

	Alcoholics	Psychotics	Ulcer	Controls
Mother	1.4	2.4	2.3	2.9
	(0 - 2.3)	(1.7 - 2.8)	(1.7 - 2.5)	(2.6 - 3.0)
Father	1.1	1.7	2.2	2.6
	(0 - 1.7)	(0 - 2.6)	(1.7 - 2.7)	(0 - 3.0)
Sibs	1.2	2.1	2.3	2.7
	(0 - 3.0)	(0 - 3.0)	(1.8 - 2.8)	(0 - 3.0)
Over-all Means	1.2	2.1	2.3	2.7

The mean rating across all stimulus variables was computed for each of the three stimulus categories for each subject. Subjects were then compared by pairs using the binomial expansion. Table 8 shows the P values obtained. It will be noted that the controls are significantly differentiated from the three experimental groups for all three stimulus categories. The alcoholics are differentiated from the psychotics and ulcer patients for Mother and Father but not for Siblings. No significant differences were found between the psychotics and ulcer patients.

The findings suggest that the reported behaviors of the Mother, Father and Siblings of the experimental subjects dur-

TABLE 8—*P Values for Data Summarized in Table 7*

	Alcoholics	Psychotics	Ulcer	Controls
Mother				
Alcoholics	—	.001	.002	.001
Psychotics			.17	.001
Ulcer				.02
Controls				—
Father				
Alcoholics	—	.03	.002	.01
Psychotics			.09	.01
Ulcer				.002
Controls				—
Sibs				
Alcoholics	—	.36	.17	.01
Psychotics			.36	.02
Ulcer				.05
Controls				—

ing the first ten years of life were more deviant than those of the controls. Thus, the Fathers and Mothers of the experimental subjects were reported as showing little affection (as behaviorally defined in the text), whereas the parents of the control subjects showed affection according to expectancy. The Mothers and Fathers of the skid-row alcoholics were reported as exhibiting the greatest deviancy of the four groups. The data indicate little difference between the deviancies of the parents and siblings of the psychotics and ulcer cases. The data are unanimous in suggesting the importance of *Father*, as well as Mother. We feel that, at present, the data are of such a preliminary nature that further statements concerning the differential effects of stimulus categories and variables should not be made.

TABLE 9—*University of Tennessee Deprivation Scale Scores*

	Alcoholics ($N=10$)	Psychotics ($N=10$)	Ulcer ($N=9$)	Control ($N=10$)
Mean	11.7	9.9	8.2	3.7
Range	8 - 14	6 - 14	3 - 13	2 - 6

As indicated above the University of Tennessee Deprivation Scale was applied to the cross-sectional status of all subjects. Table 9 shows that the alcoholics obtain the highest scores and that the psychotics and ulcer cases are, again, intermediate between them and the controls. Tables 7 and 9 suggest a very interesting, very tentative hypothesis. Note that the alcoholics reported extreme deviancy on the part of Mother, Father and Siblings during the first ten years of life. Note, also, that the alcoholics report current extreme environmental deprivation. In contrast to these findings, the psychotics and ulcer cases report much less deviancy on the part of the parents and siblings during the first ten years of life. Nevertheless, reports of their current status show them to be more like the alcoholics than the controls. The very tentative notion suggested, here, is that current "stress" may be as significantly related to duodenal ulcer and psychosis as the characteristics of important people in the early environment.

One obvious possibility suggests itself at this point, namely, the relationship between reported characteristics of important people in the subjects' early life and current functioning as assessed by the U. T. Deprivation Scale. In order to estimate this possibility, over-all means for each subject were computed using only the ratings of Mother and Father. For each experimental group and the control group these over-all means by subjects were summed and a grand mean computed. Similarly, a grand mean was computed for the Deprivation Scale scores. All cases were sorted as above or below the grand mean on the two measures, the over-all rating by subjects on Mother and Father, and Deprivation Scale scores. These were now tallied in two-by-two tables contrasting each experimental group with the controls. Table 10 shows the results obtained. It will be noticed that the relationship for the alcoholic study is relatively high. This finding is expected since the alcoholics were extremely deprived both in their early life and currently, whereas the controls were not deprived in either measure. Interest focuses on the differences between the alcoholics, on the one hand, and the psychotic and ulcer cases, on the other, in Table 10. The predictability of current deprivation based

TABLE 10—*The Relationship Between Ratings of Mother and Father and Scores on the U.T. Deprivation Scale*
(Scores above the grand mean on the Deprivation Scale and below the grand mean on the ratings for mother and father indicate "deprivation.")

			Grand Mean of Ratings of mother and father	
Grand			Above	Below
		Above	0	10
Mean	Alcoholics			
		Below	9	1
			Phi. = .89	
of				
Deprivation	Psychotics	Above	2	7
		Below	9	2
Scale			Phi. = .60	
		Above	2	6
Scores	Ulcer			
		Below	8	2
			Phi. = .55	

on early deprivation, as defined, seems to be much less for these latter two groups than for the alcoholics. This finding is in accord with our previously stated notion about the possibility that current "stress" may be a more important factor in psychoses and ulcer than in alcoholism.

We are extremely conscious of the fallibility of findings such as these. The primary purpose in reporting them has been to illustrate method.

REFERENCES

Annual Report, Alcoholism Research Project, Knoxville, University of Tennessee Psychological Service Center, 1959.

Davis, H. C., Jr.: A comparative study of the experiential characteristics of a group of alcoholic and non-alcoholic subjects. Doctoral dissertation, University of Tennessee, 1959.

Mullen, F. G., Jr.: A comparative study of the experiential characteristics of a group of peptic ulcer and non-ulcer subjects. Doctoral dissertation, University of Tennessee, 1959.

Pascal, G. R., and Jenkins, W. O.: A study of the early environment of workhouse inmates alcoholics and its relationship to adult behavior. Quart. J. Stud. Alcohol *21:* 40-50, 1960.

A Final Word 13

It is our contention that research involving intact organisms should begin with systematic observation of the gross behavior of the organism. It is only in this way that limiting characteristics of organisms can be learned and target populations established. In extreme cases such a concern becomes obvious. Thus, the sex of a pigeon can only be determined, in the intact organisms, by egg-laying behavior or copulation. Without knowledge of the gross characteristics of the organism, variables appropriate to the study of behavioral phenomena cannot be identified. This point even applies when we consider physiological studies. Thus, extirpation of the occipital area in animals primarily responding to visual cues is quite a different matter from the same extirpation in auditory animals. Whereas the observation of gross behavior is quite common at the infrahuman level prior to research, it is most uncommon in human research.

In considering the human species as a target population we can, for some purposes, treat them as a single population in that they have many characteristics in common. However, for most behavioral investigations we need to limit the target population to well-defined, homogeneous groups. It is our belief that we can only establish well-defined groups by studying the behavioral characteristics of individuals. Unless study is made of the gross behavior of the individual, important variables which will bias research data will be unknown. Thus, if the purpose of the research is to study locomotion, individuals with one leg will constitute a different target population from those with two legs. To take a more subtle case, if the assumption is made that suggestibility is related to deferential behavior of a subject toward a figure of authority, then research with pain thresholds will yield distorted results if this response variable is not controlled. In such a case, those subjects exhibiting much deferential behavior might well constitute a different target population from those exhibiting lesser amounts of this behavior.

Recently, there has been much public discussion concerning the possible relationship between smoking and the incidence of cancer of the lungs. In the studies reported in newspapers and magazines, gross behavioral data describing the research populations have not been reported. The impact of such behavioral parameters as early and current environmental deprivation on smoking, per se, and lung cancer is unknown. For instance, what is the relationship between adult smoking behavior and early life experiences? Gross variables potentially related to human behavior need to be controlled. We will not know whether they effect the dependent variable in question without experimental test. This sequence of events is necessary if we are to arrive at well-defined, homogeneous target populations. This sequence of events is also necessary if we are to control, insofar as the state of knowledge permits, gross variables which systematically bias the data.

Careful matching of subjects is usually required in small-number research. A variable such as heterosexual attractiveness, which is usually not considered in matching procedures, is potentially capable of introducing bias in the data. We do not, as yet, know if any relationship exists between gross behavior and degrees of heterosexual attractiveness. Selection cannot be applied to the process of matching without knowledge of the behavioral characteristics of the target populations. (There are, of course, obvious limits to both controlling and matching. Thus, matching can, in the extreme, be carried to the point at which the behaviors of interest are erased.)

The point we are making here is that in any scientific inquiry it is essential that the characteristics of the subjects under investigation be grossly known. Without such information variability is maximized and the acquistion of lawful relationships is retarded. We feel that the use of the P-J Scales will not only result in establishing more homogeneous target populations, but in better matching and decreased variability.

APPENDICES

Interview Guide

PASCAL-JENKINS BEHAVIORAL SCALES

(This interview guide is not to be used without thorough knowledge of the supporting text which deals with the qualifications of the Examiner and methodology.)

Description of the Subject. All subjects are identified as follows: (If subject is a minor include pertinent data about parents.)

code number	residence
sex	cultural background (subject's
age	origin, vocation and status
race	of parents, etc.)
education	socio-economic status
religion	intellectual level
vocation	physical description
marital status	physical condition
children (no., age, sex)	mental status
siblings (no., age, sex)	locale of interviews
income	source of information

Basic Measures. The following measures are to be attempted for all behaviors.

frequency	amount
latency	variety
rate	conditions
intensity	direction
duration	efficiency

Obtaining Information from Collaterals. In interviewing collaterals to obtain data about a subject, the pertinent parts of these Scales are used. Also, additional information is obtained, depending on the subject and the nature of the investigation. Thus, if the parents of a subject are interviewed concerning the early years of life of the subject, information is obtained about the family circumstances prior to birth, the course of pregnancy and the details of birth. Thereafter, the parents are queried using the entire P-J Scales. BIs are gathered, as in all data-collecting.

Scale A: Stimulus Categories

I. Known Organisms as Stimuli (S) (Obtain orienting information for each stimulus, e.g., age, education, vocation, race, religion and physical description.)

S1.1 Paternal grandmother
S1.2 Paternal grandfather
S1.3 Maternal grandmother
S1.4 Maternal grandfather
S2.1 Mother
S2.2 Father
S2.3 Additional parents
S3.1 Oldest sib
S3.2 Next oldest sib, etc.
S4.1 First peer, same sex
S4.2 Second peer, same sex, etc.
S5.1 First peer, opposite sex
S5.2 Second peer, opposite sex, etc.
S6.1 First older person, same sex
S6.2 Second older person, same sex, etc.
S7.1 First older person, opposite sex
S7.2 Second older person, opposite sex, etc.
S8.1 First younger person, same sex
S8.2 Second younger person, same sex, etc.
S9.1 First younger person, opposite sex
S9.2 Second younger person, opposite sex, etc.
S10.1 First spouse
S10.2 Second spouse, etc.
S11.1 Oldest child
S11.2 Next oldest child, etc.
S12.1 First animal
S12.2 Second animal, etc.

Variables for known Organisms as stimuli. (BIs should be collected about the behaviors of the known stimuli using these variables as a guide. See the text for a definition of the variables.)

1. Frequency of Contact
2. Play Activities
3. Displays of Affection
4. Providing Behavior
5. Restraints
6. Physical Punishment
7. Verbal Punishment
8. Intellectual Behavior
9. Status
10. Social Behavior
11. Religious Behavior
12. Physical Health
13. Compatibility
14. Role
15. Variability of Habitat
16. Sexual Behavior
17. Deviant Behavior

II. Other Known Stimulus Categories. (See text for a definition of these categories.)

S13.1 First school
S13.2 Second school, etc.
S14.1 First job
S14.2 Second job, etc.
S15.1 First subculture
S15.2 Second subculture, etc.
S16.1 First physical environment
S16.2 Second physical environment, etc.
S17.1 First unavoidable illness or accident
S17.2 Second unavoidable illness or accident, etc.

Variables for other Stimulus Categories. (BIs should be collected for each of these stimuli using these variables as a guide. See the text for a definition of these variables.)

18. Prestige
19. Social Demands
20. Intellectual Demands
21. Physical Demands
22. Religious Demands
23. Financial Demands
24. Restrictiveness
25. Danger

Scale B: Responses to Known Stimulus Categories

I. S-R Behaviors. S-R Behaviors are reactions by the subject to specific variables of the stimulus categories, e.g., S-R12.1-3 is the response *by the subject* to Displays of Affection on the part of the first animal. S-R behaviors are to be obtained for each of the variables for all stimulus categories. *The Examiner is reminded that for Stimulus categories other than organisms this is all the information on the response side that will be obtained.* If it is desired to code this part of the scales, coding is as follows:

S-R1.1-1 Responses by the subject to Frequency of Contact on the part of the Paternal Grandmother.

S-R1.1-2 Responses by the subject to Activities on the part of the Paternal Grandmother, etc.

II. Other Responses to Known Stimulus Categories (R-S). For each known organism as a stimulus BIs must be collected for the classes of behaviors indicated by the following variables. They are behaviors *initiated by the subject* toward the stimulus and thus differing from S-R behaviors. See the text for a definition of these response variables.

1. Adience-abience
2. Displays of Affection
3. Helpful Behavior
4. Companionship Activity
5. Providing Behavior
6. Copying Behavior
7. Dependent Behavior
8. Competitive Behavior
9. Physical Aggression
10. Verbal Aggression
11. Restraints
12. Sexual Behavior
13. Fear Behavior
14. Deviant Behavior

Scale C: Operant Responses (The basic measures are the principal variables. See the text for additional cues to data-gathering.)

OR1.0 Oral Habits
OR1.1 Eating
OR1.2 Drinking
OR1.3 Smoking

OR2.0 Sleeping
OR2.1 Sleeping
OR2.2 Dreaming

OR3.0 Elimination
OR3.1 Defecation
OR3.2 Urination

OR4.0 Cleanliness
OR4.1 Body Proper
OR4.2 Hands and Face
OR4.3 Sex Organs
OR4.4 Teeth
OR4.5 Clothes
OR4.6 Living Quarters
OR4.7 Food and Drink

OR5.0 Motility
OR5.1 Gross Bodily Movements
OR5.2 Fine Movements
OR5.3 Verbal Behavior

OR6.0 Health
OR6.1 Attention to Physical Well-Being
OR6.2 Illnesses and Accidents
OR6.3 Menstruation

OR7.0 Sexual Behavior
OR7.1 Sexual Seeking Behavior
OR7.2 Heterosexual Behavior
OR7.3 Sexual Behavior — Other

OR8.0 Social Behavior (General)
OR8.1 Social Play
OR8.2 Public Behavior
OR8.3 Companionship Seeking Activity (nonsexual)

OR9.0 Social Behavior (Specific)
OR9.1 Behavior Toward Unknown People (younger and older people, same and opposite sex, peers, superiors and inferiors.)
OR9.2 Behavior Toward Unknown Animals

OR10.0 Conforming Behavior
OR10.1 Social
OR10.2 Intellectual

OR11.0 Level of Responding
OR11.1 Alertness to Cue Change
OR11.2 Response to Stress
OR11.3 Work Level

OR12.0 Other nonoccupational Activities
OR12.1 Hobbies and Avocations
OR12.2 Solitary Behavior
OR12.3 Hoarding Behavior
OR12.4 Driving Behavior

Illustrative Data to Show Methods of Tabulation and Data Analysis

II

The table in this appendix was prepared by selecting actual data from our study of workhouse alcoholics. For purposes of simplification, we have used only one stimulus category (mother) and selected stimulus variables. As can be seen the raw data, by variables, were tabulated for the stimulus category. The next step was to average the ratings across rows (variables) in order to accomplish the over-all analysis. The column on the far right represents the combined average of ratings for variables by subject pairs. It can be seen that the mean ratings for the experimental and control subjects are nonoverlapping. For every pair, the mean rating of the control exceeded that of the experimental subject. For 10 out of 10 events in the same direction the binomial yields a probability of .001. This finding, then, allows us to enter the individual columns with some degree of confidence. If this finding had not been significant, it would have cast some doubt on findings attributable to individual columns. Our next step, then, was to count, by variables, the number of times the control's rating exceeds that of the experimental for pairs in which the ND category does *not* appear. Thus, in the column for Activities, the analysis was based on only seven pairs, with no reversals. The binomial for seven events in the same direction gives a P value of .008. A similar analysis was accomplished for the other columns, as shown in the table. One additional point, when ties occurred they were split between experimental and control subjects.

From the illustrative data it can be seen that a summary table can be prepared showing the findings either by stimulus categories (mother, father, peers, etc.) or by individual variables across all stimulus categories. Such a table will be found in the text in Chapter 12 showing the findings with workhouse alcoholics.

111

APPENDIX II: Ratings for Subject's Mother

Subject Pairs	Activities		Physical Punish		Displays Affects		Religious Behavior		Average Ratings All Variables	
	E	C	E	C	E	C	E	C	E	C
1	0	ND	0	ND	0	ND	0	3	0	3.0
2	1	ND	2	2	1	2	2	3	1.5	2.3
3	2	3	1	3	1	3	ND	3	1.3	3.0
4	0	3	0	3	0	3	0	3	0	3.0
5	1	3	1	3	1	3	1	3	1.0	3.0
6	1	2	2	3	2	3	3	3	2.0	2.8
7	1	3	1	3	1	3	ND	2	1.0	2.8
8	1	3	1	3	2	3	1	3	1.2	3.0
9	ND	3	1	2	1	3	ND	3	1.0	2.8
10	1	3	3	2	2	3	1	2	1.8	2.5
$\overline{X}$	1.0	2.9	1.3	2.7	1.2	2.9	1.1	2.9	1.1	2.8
Number of Pairs	7		9		9		7		10	
P value	.008		.055		.002		.035		.001	

Illustrative Interview Material   III

This appendix presents verbatim excerpts from interviews with one subject, a female college student. The focus is on obtaining data about the stimulus variable, Displays of Affection from Mother, S2.1-3, for the first 10 years of life of the subject.

Much background material is omitted from these excerpts but enough is given to illustrate how BIs are obtained in practice. There follow six BIs bearing on the variable Displays of Affection by Mother toward our subject. These are followed by an example of what is often mistaken for a BI, behavioral information which is not anchored to a particular event. Thereafter, the use of simple relaxation in obtaining additional BIs is illustrated. Finally, corroborating information from a collateral, Father, is presented.

BI 1

E: Well, you say you remember your mother when she would come and pick you up at school. Do you remember any one such time, I mean any one time. Just think back now. Remember her picking you up?

S: I remember her picking me once in the second grade.

E: All right, then, you were about how old then?

S: Seven.

E: Seven, all right. You were at school?

S: Yes.

E: And, you left the school room by yourself, you mean.

S: I . . . I, yes, they thought I had pink eye or something and she . . .

E: The teacher had called your mother and did she come into the class-room and pick you up? Where did she pick you up?

S: No, I think I was standing outside waiting on her. Out by the door.

E: By the door?

S: Yes.

E: Did she drive up?

S: No, my aunt brought her.

E: Your aunt was driving the car? And your mother was sitting with her?

S: Yes.

E: And then what happened?

S: Then I ran to the car. I was feeling bad. I really didn't have . . . wasn't sick. But they thought I was.

E: You ran to the car, all right. Then what happened?

S: Got in the car.

E: Where did you get in the car? In the back?

S: Probably.

E: Probably, you don't remember?

S: I don't . . . Well, I know that when my aunt drives no one — hardly ever three people sit in the front, and so . . .

E: I see. What did your mother say or do when she saw you?

S: She asked me if I had the pink eye and I said . . . I remember my eyes were red and it was because something had happened at home that morning and I had been crying. And thought that was what it was.

E: Yes.

S: Of course, there wasn't any way they could tell, but mother and I knew. She asked me how I felt and then we went home.

E: Did she touch you or anything?

S: No, she probably . . . I can't remember. No, I don't remember her doing anything that time.

BI 2

E: What's another early memory you have of your mother, S?

S: I went to camp, but I don't know when that was. I remember then when they came to pick me up, I was overjoyed to see them.

E: You were at camp?

S: Yes.

E: Can you remember what grade of school you were in?

S: It was after — it was probably the fourth or third.

E: Third or fourth grade? Uh-huh. Well, let's see. The third grade would make you about nine, wouldn't it? You started to school when you were six?

S: When I was five. My birthday is in November.

E: When you were five. Oh, I see — you would have been eight then. Now tell me about that.

S: Well, I remember we were having a banquet inside the room. They always have a going away thing, you know. And Mother and Daddy were waiting on me outside when I got through. And I remember running outside and seeing — Daddy was out of the car, and I remember I ran up and he said I practically knocked him down.

E: Uh-huh.

S: Mother was in the car and I kissed her.

E: You kissed her? Did she kiss you first — back?

S: I'd say she did; she does anyway.

BI 3

E: Well, how did you go to bed? Did she go too — Did you go to bed at the same time?

S: Yes.

E: All right, what happened? Did she say you were going to sleep with her that night?

S: No. I wanted to. We lived on a highway where there was quite a bit of traffic and there were quite a few accidents and I didn't like to sleep in the front bedroom by myself anyway. And so, when Daddy wasn't there I jumped at the opportunity to sleep back there. And — I mean — she was — I mean I guess she would have asked me to if I hadn't of just taken it for granted that I would sleep back there.

E: You just took it for granted.

S: Yes.

E: Well, what did you do? Did you undress in your own room?

S: No. The bathroom.

E: In the bathroom?

S: Yes.

E: Did she say, 'It's time for you to go to bed now, S?'

S: No, she never did. I don't think so.

E: You don't remember her saying that.

S: No.

E: You just both went to bed together.

S: Yes.

E: And you undressed in the bathroom?

S: Yes, we always — I always took a bath right before I went to bed.

E: Did you that night?

S: Yes.

E: By yourself?

S: Yes. I never — well — I can't remember when I didn't. I mean, I know I didn't all the time but . . .

E: Then what did you put on? Pajamas? Or a nightgown?

S: Pajamas.

E: Pajamas. And then when you got in your mother's bed, were you in there first or she first?

S: She was probably there first. She usually was.

E: She was in there first.

S: She used to always go to bed earlier.

E: And what would happen? What would happen when you got in bed then?

S: She just said good night . . .

E: Did she kiss you?

S: No, I don't think so.

E: Did she snuggle up to you or something?

S: I don't think so, not that I can remember.

BI 4

E: Uh-huh. I mean what happened? You remember — think of one time now, S. So you and your cousin are at home together, your home. Then your mother said go to bed?

S: Yes.

E: She went to bed at the same time?

S: Yes.

E: About what time would this be, about?

S: Oh, about 9:30 or 10:00.

E: About 9:30 or 10:00. Then you undressed in the bathroom. Take a bath again?

S: Yes.

E: Just like you usually do?

S: Just like . . . Yes.

E: Then you went and laid down. Did you lay between your mother and your cousin or on the outside?

S: I usually slept on the outside. Mother slept on one outside and I did on the other, because my cousin was younger than I was and she was scared.

E: She was scared?

S: Yes.

E: Then what happened? Did you just say good-night?

S: No. Well, my cousin ran around for good-night kisses and got — I mean I did, too. She always did it when she was there, and I did, too.

E: You did it when she was there?

S: But I don't remember too much whenever just us were there by ourselves.

E: When you were by yourself — not. Uh-huh.

BI 5

E: Well, can you remember any night when you went to sleep by yourself?

S: Yes, I can remember when I was just learning to sleep in there by myself. I used to have a room — a bed in mother and daddy's bedroom. That was before my room — I mean I never did want to go in there because of the traffic and all. It was pretty loud and it was pretty hard to sleep. And I remember learning to sleep in there. 'Cause I remember lots of nights I would get up and go back into the other bedroom.

E: And sleep in your little bed, you mean?

S: Yes.

E: Uh-huh. Well, do you remember your mother putting you to bed there?

S: In my room you mean? Yes, I remember once particularly when she put me and went to bed with me.

E: Went to bed with you there? Uh-huh. She laid beside you for a while?

S: Yes.

E: Uh-huh. Did she do anything? Did she hold you?

S: She kissed me good-night that night.

E: That time she kissed you good-night.

S: I guess for reassurance.

BI 6

E: Well, did you see your mother? What happened?

S: We were all laughing about Daddy forgot me.

E: He forgot you? Uh-huh.

S: Yes.

E: And did your mother say something when she saw you?

S: She said that she knew that he was home early because he didn't come by for me. She said that when she saw that I wasn't in the car she wondered where I was because I didn't usually just leave without telling one of them.

E: She just said hello to you, you mean?

S: Hello. Uh-huh.

E: And then what was she doing when you came back?

S: She was sitting out on the — we had a big old flight of stairs that went up the back of house and she was sitting up there with my aunt.

E: Sitting upstairs?

S: Yes. Up on the steps outside.

E: Up on the steps. And then what happened?

S: We ran upstairs. She asked me about school and everything.

Behavioral information is obtained in the excerpt below, but not a BI. It is not a particular stimulus-response sequence anchored in time.

E: Did you say good-bye to mother when leaving for school? How did you say good-bye?

S: I usually kissed her good-bye.

E: Kissed her good-bye. Did she kiss you?

S: Yes.

E: Did you go and find her wherever she was?

S: She was usually in the kitchen. We had to go through the kitchen to get out. But if she wasn't, I did.

E: Would she come look for you to kiss you good-bye?

S: I don't remember. I remember every time we left she was standing there in the kitchen. If she was going to work she went with us. I remember kissing her good-bye.

> *Again, behavioral information is obtained but no BI.*
> *(Later, see below, a BI bearing on these reports*
> *is obtained under simple relaxation.)*

E: Uh-huh. Did she ever read to you?

S: Uh-huh. She used to read — well, not so much reading — I can't remember so much reading . . . She used to tell me a lot of stories.

E: Tell you stories?

S: Uh-huh. I remember that night, I don't remember how old I was but I can remember, I asked her to tell me the story of the Three Little Bears. I must have been six or seven years old because we thought, I laughed because she though it was unusual that I would want to hear a child, a fairytale, so to speak, like that. *(This is an incomplete BI.)*

E: Uh-huh.

S: But she used to make up a lot of stories and tell me.

E: Uh-huh. Can you remember any times like that when she did?

S: I remember she used to tell about when she was a little girl and they lived near where the gypsies or where people like that — or she would tell me they did — where the gypsies came in and out and how they stole things out of her grandmother's house. I remember that particularly.

E: Do you remember the night she told you that?

S: No, because she would tell me that several times because I liked it and would ask her to tell it again.

E: Do you remember any one time when she said that?

S: No. I don't believe so.

E: Can't remember any particular incident?

S: No, I can't.

> *The use of simple relaxation in obtaining a BI about Displays*
> *of Affection is illustrated.*
> *Note that it is not a BI*
> *until a particular S-R sequence is obtained.*

E: Well, S, let's try something to see if I can help you remember. Want to?

S: O.K.

E: You go lie on the couch.

S: What?

E: Lie there on the couch. Just lie there and relax, S.

S: O.K.

E: Make yourself as comfortable as you can be. All right, S. Now can you stretch right out?

S: Oh, yes.

E: Put your hands to your side. Now are you comfortable?

S: Uh-huh.

E: Nice and comfortable. It's all safe here, S.

S: Yes, I know.

E: Now, S, I want you to take a nice deep breath. Deep breath, I'm not going to hypnotize you so don't worry about that. Take a real deep breath, deep breath. Draw in as much air as you can and hold it tight. Make your diaphragm good and tight, you see?

S: Uh-huh.

E: And then exhale, slowly and relax yourself. See? Did you exhale?

S: Uh-huh.

E: See how it feels?

S: Uh-huh.

E: All right. Try it again, now. Real deep breath. Hold it tight, and then slowly exhale. Feel yourself relax. Can you feel yourself relaxing? O.K. Once more when you're ready, S. Deep breath, hold it tight. Now exhale and relax, that's it. Nice and easy. That's fine. I want you to get to feel nice and relaxed. Once more when you're ready. Real deep breath, deep breath. Hold it tight now, tight, and exhale and relax. You feel real relaxed now, S?

S: Yes.

E: Just relax, nice and easy. Take another deep breath now. Hold it tight and relax. Feel yourself relaxing all over your body. That's good. Now feel relaxed and listen to me. Try to follow along with me. I want you to try to imagine a kind of relaxing that starts in your toes and feel it spreading throughout your foot and feel the muscles in your foot relaxing. Feel it spread up over your ankles slowly up the calves of your legs through the muscles, making them nice and loose. Feel it spread up over your knees, slowly upward over the thighs, loosing the muscles, relaxing more and more. Feel it coming over your buttocks. Feel all those muscles from your waist down all relaxed. Can you feel your lower extremeties relaxed, S? (S nods.)

E. That's good. Now try to imagine that same feeling in your hands. Let the muscles in your hands loosen up. Let them relax, feel relaxed. Feel both hands relaxed, feel all those muscles loose. Feel it come up over your wrists, slowly through your forearm loosening up the muscles, relax. Over your elbows, up to your upper arm muscles. Feel them loosening, nice and relaxed, all those muscles. Up over your shoulders, all those muscles in your shoulders relaxing. Now it's creeping up to your neck muscles. Feel your neck loose and relaxed. All right, relax. Feel it spread up over your face, your jaw muscles. Let them loosen up. Feel it over your forehead, your eyebrows. Just try to feel nice and relaxed, S. Just close your eyes. It's all safe here. Just try to relax.

S: I'm afraid I'll go to sleep.

E: That's all right. If you feel drowsy, let yourself feel drowsy. That's all right. Now feel relaxed. It's all right. Just relax, nice and relaxed. Nice and comfortable. Real comfortable, nice and comfortable and relaxed. Drowsy and relaxed. Real relaxed. Nice and relaxed. Let yourself relax all over. All right relax all over, S. Let's go back in time now. I want you to remember when you were a small, small child. Feel nice and relaxed. Take yourself back in time when you were a small child. Try to remember when you were a small child. Imagine when the tables looked big and the chairs looked big and your parents were big and tall. Can you imagine that, S? Nod your head. (S nods.)

E: I want you to try to visualize a scene when you were on your mother's lap.

S: I remember sitting on her lap when she would read to me.

E: When she would read to you. How would you get on her lap? Did she get you or did you climb up there?

S: She put me there when I was small but I remember just going and getting on her lap lots of times.

E: Do you remember anything about when you were sitting on her lap? Did she put her arms around you to hold you?

S: Yes, she put one arm ... well, to hold the book. (*This statement particularizes the event.*)

The following excerpts show, again, the use of simple relaxation in obtaining a BI. In the first section an attempt is made to obtain data concerning Physical Punishment by Father. However, no BIs were remembered. In the second section, after the subject has been helped to relax, a BI is obtained.

Before Relaxation

E: Well, about how often would your father spank you?

S: I remember him spanking me quite a few times. He always did it with a little stick, I mean a little switch.

E: A little switch. Do you remember the kind of things he would spank you for, S?

S: I can't remember anything right now.

E: All right. Nothing comes to mind why he would spank you but you remember it being quite often when you were a little child.

S: Yes.

E: Do you remember any particular time he spanked you.

S: No. I remember he always took me into the bathroom and stood me up on a little stool and switched my legs real hard.

E: Took you in the bathroom, stood you on a stool so he wouldn't have to bend over.

S: I guess. I don't know, but it hurt.

E: You can't remember one particular time, S?

S: No, I don't.

During Relaxation

E: Uh-huh. Think back now, way back. I want you to remember your father. Can you remember about your father? What's happening?

S: I guess I was thinking about him whipping me.

E: Thinking about him whipping you?

S: Uh-huh.

E: Why did he spank you? Did you do something?

S: I remember once him taking me out of the room when he had company and taking me back to the bathroom and whipping me but I don't know what for.

E: You remember him taking you out of the living room and taking you back to the bathroom and whipping you.

S: Yes.

E: And then what happened. Just relax, S. Nice and relaxed. Relaxed now. Do you remember why he whipped you?

S: I think it was something I did that he didn't want me to do. I mean he told me to do something and I didn't do it, like sit down or get out of the middle of the room or something like that.

E: Something that you didn't do, so he spanked you.

S: Yes.

E: Get out of the room, or something like that. I see.

The following information was obtained in an interview with the father of our subject. It is presented verbatic. It can be seen that although an attempt was made to obtain BIs, they were not always forthcoming. Nevertheless, data corroborating the subject's report were elicited.

An example of behavioral data — not a BI

E: Did your wife kiss your daughter good-bye in the morning when your daughter left for school?

S: Yes.

E: Was it a fairly typical pattern?

S: Yes.

E: When she kissed her, did she lay her hands on her, pat her or something like that?

S: Well, it was more or less just a good-bye kiss. No show of unusual loving affection, you know what I mean. She never was much to display it that way.

E: What did she do? Kiss your daughter on the cheek and your daughter kissed her back?

S: Yes. These things are kind of hard for me to remember. I have to think back and recall all that.

Incomplete BI on Displays of Affection

E: Do you remember anything about your wife's behavior when you went to pick your daughter up at the summer camp — that summer when she was ten?

S: Nothing unusual, just a happy meeting.

E: What happened on first contact?

S: Mother gave her a hug and kiss.

E: How about yourself and your daughter in that situation. Did she hug and kiss you?

S: Oh, yes. She was always affectionate, although not excessively so. She was always glad to see me as well as her mother.

Corroborating data obtained from father bearing on a BI reported by the subject. This is not a BI.

E: When your daughter got older and was preparing for bed, did her mother do anything special with your daughter, reading books to her, etc.?

S: Yes. She would read these child's books —"Little Red Riding Hood."

E: That sounds familiar.

S: Oh, yes, sure.

E: Do you remember how — could you reconstruct the scene? Could you remember how the situation looked, what your wife did . . .?

S: Well, that's pretty hard.

E: Just wondered where your daughter was — your wife.

S: Yes. Well, I believe she would sit with her in a chair before she would actually put her to bed, and read those things to her. Of course, my daughter was quite an active little youngster, she was sort of the tomboyish type of girl and she was up and down and jumping around in between times. But, she would read those to her in the chair on her lap.

E: Your daughter on your wife's lap?

S: **Yes.**

E: Did your wife — did you see your wife sort of spontaneously hug or pat your daughter? Do you recall?

S: Well, yes, yes, she would. But not too much show of affection. But what I mean she would always take care of her and pet her and love her when the child would come to her.

A BI obtained from father on Providing Behavior by Mother toward the subject. Although the data are not directly pertinent to the variable Displays of Affection, they are related to it.

E: Do you remember any particular incident where your daughter had a bad fall, illness or something like that — where your wife exhibited affection?

S: Yes, I remember when she was just — I guess about 6 or 8 months old — she very near had pneumonia and my wife was very concerned. We were at her sister's home and she wouldn't bring the baby home. She was afraid to bring her out, because it was during a snowy season that we were having at that time. She stayed with the baby during the night and I went on home. She stayed with her and took care of her for two or three days until she was sure that she was well.

E: Did she stay in the same room?

S: Yes, she did.

E: She stayed with her pretty much night and day?

S: Yes.

E: Good. And she didn't bring her home then until . . .

S: No, not until she felt safe about her physical condition.

Index